-to the ghosts of Bodie

"To Speak of the Dead Is To Make Them Live Again"

Egyptian Saying

1934 and 1937 Calendars

Discovering Bodie

Second Edition

Nick Gariaeff

Gilroy, CA

Copyright 2011, Nick Gariaeff. All rights reserved.

No part of this publication can be reproduced, stored in a retrieval system, or transmitted in any form, or by any means, electronic, mechanical, photocopying, or otherwise without the prior permission of the publishers and/ or the authors.

Photographed, researched, written, and designed by Nick Gariaeff

Published by Nick Gariaeff, Gilroy, CA
Visit website at www.discoveringbodie.com

ISBN 978-0-9843634-1-4

Library of Congress Control Number: 2011918959

Second Edition

Printed on Demand in the United States of America
on Acid Free Paper

Forward

The first time I photographed the abandoned mining camp of Bodie was in 1968. A photographer friend knew I enjoyed photographing abandoned homes and dilapidated barns. He suggested that the ghost town of Bodie would be interesting to photograph. He was right!

I generally photographed Bodie several times a year. I would schedule a day trip when visiting relatives in Carson City. For many years I photographed Bodie without thought to the people who lived there. I made it a point not to read books about Bodie, or learn about the mining operations, buildings, make of cars - anything. It was just a place to wander about and photograph. I always thought my best photographs were created when I didn't consciously think about what I was doing. I still do. I believe the unconscious mind can process the sense of the surrounding environment and react to it artistically much better than if one tried to stage a particular outcome.

As time went on, curiosity got the best of me. I wondered why I was attracted to the place, and what the photographs meant. People would ask me questions about the Bodie, thinking I must be an expert because I spent a considerable amount of time there. I could not answer - I had no idea! Bodie was a puzzle. I started wondering what was real, and what was staged. Who were these people? From where did they come from and where did they go? I started reading the California State Park brochure for the first time, and then all the books about Bodie I could get my hands on. The more I read, the more fascinating the town and its people became.

Eventually, I started doing research on some of the inhabitants using online census records, and going through old newspapers on microfilm. I started exchanging e-mail with relatives of some of the Bodie descendants. Vacation time was spent in the vault of the Recorder's Office and upstairs in the Mono County Museum in Bridgeport, California, to search wonderful old bound volumes for property, marriage, death, and tax records. I became obsessed with Bodie. It became clear it was my destiny to produce a book which included both my photographs, and the information which I had gathered about the people who lived there. It seemed as though I had become a medium in which ghosts of the old mining camp were communicating through me. They tugged at my arm saying "read about me". Another would grab my hand, point, and say "No - find out more about him!" When I researched the people of Bodie, there would often be connections to people that had no relationship to Bodie. These people were also fascinating to research. However, the ghosts of Bodie kept pulling me back to my main focus. This book attempts to connect the images I have created over many years, and the people of Bodie I have learned about.

Nick Gariaeff, Gilroy 2010

List of Photographs

1937 Chevrolet	Front Cover
1934 and 1937 Calendars	ii
Bodie Graveyard Entrance	1
President Garfield Monument	4
Wooden Pipe - Bodie Museum	5
Bodie Overflow Reservoir	6
Bank Ruins	7
J. S. Cain House	8
Bank Safe	9
Bodie School	10
Church Detail	11
Methodist Church	12
Methodist Church Interior	13
Graveyard Fence	14
Railroad Depot and Water Tower	15
Moonrise	16
Miller Table and Chairs	17
Miller House Kitchen	18
Miller House Bedroom	19
Miller House Doorway	20
Boone & Wright Store Window	21
Boone & Wright General Store	22
Path to Boone & Wright Store	23
Boone Feed and Tack Room	24
Bodie Garage	25
Shell Service Station	26
Johl House - Bodie	28
Lottie Johl - Bodie Museum	29
Sewing Machine	30
Johl Kitchen	31
Johl House Interior	32
Checkers	33
Johl House Stove	34
Lottie Johl Grave	35
Johl House Chair	36
Johl 1893 World's Fair Glass	37
Washington Portrait - Lottie Johl House	38
Pagdin Grave	39
Donnelly House	40
Sam Leon Bar and Barbershop	42
Sam Leon's Bar	44
Model A Ford by Sam Leon's Bar	46
Bodie Shoe Shine	47
Barber Chair	48
Assay Equipment	49
Clouds - I.O.O.F. Building and Dechambeau Hotel	50
Standard Mill	51
1925 Nash by the "La Belle Beauty Shop"	52
Burkham House on Mill Street	54
Child's Grave - Bodie Cemetery	55
Seiler House Porch	56
Back of the Swazey Hotel	57
Front of the Swazey Hotel	58
Swazey Hotel	60
Dr. Street Examination Table	62
Bodie Museum Liquor Log - Soto & Goldsmith	63
The Two Graves of Rosa May	66
Bodie Morgue	67
Bodie Jail	68
Reddy House and Quill - Bodie Reenactment	69
Morning	70
Hoover House	71
Standard Mill Office	72
Indian House, Washtub, and Bird	73
Indian House	74
Kirkwood Blacksmith Shop	75
Kirkwood House	76
Todd and Conway Houses	77
Dried Hops, Conway House	78
Conway Bedroom	79
Conway Porch	80
Robert Conway Family Items	82
Turned Wooden Globe	84
Bodie Grave	Back Cover

Contents

Forward	v	Henry F. Metzger	51
Wakeman S. Bodey	1	Cecil B. Burkham	53
Terrence Brodigan	5	August Seiler	55
James Stuart Cain	7	Horace F. Swasey	57
George B. Hinkle	11	Dr. John A. Street	61
Francis M. Warrington	13	Emma Goldsmith	63
E. J. Clinton	15	Rosa May	65
Thomas Miller	17	Patrick Reddy	69
Harvey Boone	21	Theodore J. Hoover	71
Eli Johl	27	Rosie McDonald Moose	73
Annie U. Donnelly	39	M. Y. S. Kirkwood	75
Sam Leon	41	Robert Conway	77
Joe Hahner	48	References	83
August Soderling	49		

WAKEMAN S. BODEY

Wakeman S. Bodey first discovered gold in Bodie, and died in a snowstorm several months afterwards. The town was named in his honor and was later changed to Bodie. The names are confusing because every combination of (Wakeman, Waterman, Wm.) and (Bodey, Body, Bodie) and others were used. William and Bill were also used, but not in his hometown of Poughkeepsie. The book *Bodie Bonanza* by Warren A. Loose, whose father, Warren A. R. Loose, participated along with leading citizens in exhuming Bodey's grave on October 27th, 1879, several days after it was located by Judge J. G. McClinton and Joseph Wasson relates how Bodey's belt, a handmade leather scabbard riveted with spent bullet casings, and a knife were found with his remains. The handle of the knife had a woman's head on one side and a lion on the other. A silk necktie, shoe attached to his right foot, and cloth wrapping his left foot were also found (107-108). The New York *Poughkeepsie Daily Eagle* wrote of the news the day after his remains were found:

"FINDING THE BODY OF WM. S. BODEY
What Befell the Discoverer of a Famous Silver Mine. The following Associated Press dispatch was received by us late last night: SAN FRANCISCO, Oct. 27.

The remains of W. S. Bodie, the original discoverer of the Bodie Mining District, and who perished in a snow storm on November, 1859, were discovered yesterday about a mile southwest of the town of Bodie. The deceased is believed to be a native of Rochester or Poughkeepsie, New York, where he left a family."

The Poughkeepsie article, incorrectly identifying Bodey's discovery of silver instead of gold, went on to tell local facts regarding "Mr. Bodey". On October 30th, another article appeared. Sarah Bodey, his widow, was visiting her sister in New Jersey during this time. The article used the name "Waterman", perhaps a fire department nickname, instead of "Wakeman", which was used in the census records. The articles both assumed incorrectly that his body was frozen for twenty years and perfectly preserved rather than buried, and that others in the mining party were at the cabin when Bodey and Black

Bodie Graveyard Entrance

Taylor, a half Cherokee, went for supplies about 15 miles away:

> "Waterman S. Bodey was thirty years ago a resident of Poughkeepsie, a tinsmith by profession, and an industrious, hard working man. He was regarded among his fellow workers in the trade as a leader, because of his superior skill, and because of his naturally energetic disposition. He was an earnest member of the fire department and a leading Odd Fellow, and introduced some of the now prominent citizens, who were then young men, into the mysteries of that order. In 1848, the California gold fever broke out and ran wildly through the Eastern States, and a party was formed in Poughkeepsie, among who was Jacob Statter and Waterman Bodey. The big schooner Matthew Vassar was fitted out with everything necessary for a voyage, and in the fall of 1849 the latter part of adventurers bid adieu to Poughkeepsie, and in a short time were on the ocean, their route being around Cape Horn and the voyage took months of time, during which all suffered many privations.
>
> They arrived in San Francisco safely, however, and the party broke up and became scattered, each one seeking his own fortune. Bodey by hard work secured a position in a dry goods store, and afterwards went into business himself, but lost heavily. Leaving the Golden Gate City he went to seek his fortune in the mountain districts of the El Doraldo and mingled with the miners, many of whom were meeting with great luck, and unearthing fabulous sums of gold. His perseverance and energy were suddenly rewarded when he struck the surface vein of a mine which panned out gold in promising quantities, and it soon became known as the Bodey mine, when he with several others built a stone hut and commenced work.
>
> During all this time he had written regularly to his wife in this city, and had sent her money for her support. In November, 1859, the mining party found themselves threatened with starvation, and Bodey with a companion started for a settlement to buy provisions. On the return trip the two men were lost in a snow storm, and bewildered by the blinding flakes they wandered for hours in the intense cold through drifts and gulches without number. Bodey finally became delirious and his companion was forced to abandon him in order to save himself. Luckily he was but a short distance from camp, and stumbled suddenly into warmth and comfort. As soon as the exhausted man could gasp out his tale, the others started out to search for Bodey, but though they tramped around the snow all night they could not find the slightest trace of their missing leader. For twenty years therefore, a mystery has surrounded the end of Waterman Bodey, and his wife has never given up a faint hope of seeing him again. During all these years she has resided in this city, earning a scanty living as a seamstress, and enduring an accumulation of misfortunes in the successive lost of six children - some of them meeting violent deaths. One of them was drowned in the old mill pond, and another who learned his father's trade, fell from a high landing in New Brunswick, N. J., and was fatally injured."

The *New York Times* ran a similar article on October 30th, but used the name Bodie instead of Bodey.

Census records for 1850 list Wakeman S. Bodey, 36, a tinsmith, Sarah Bodey, 30, a seamstress, and children George 9, Wm 7, Ogden 4, and Mary 1. In early census years a member of a family who was away was enumerated with the family normal place of abode. In 1860, Wakeman Bodey is listed last with the family instead of first, where the head of the household was normally listed. In addition, the U.S. Federal Census Mortality Schedules, which tracked those who died within a year prior to the current census, listed Wakeman S. Bodey, a tinsmith from Poughkeepsie as having died in December of 1859 by freezing to death at age 57. His son George, who died of typhoid fever at the age of 19 is also listed. The census records indicate that both Wakeman and Sarah were born in New York. Apparently they first came to Poughkeepsie in 1843. The Poughkeepsie Village Directory of 1843 first lists Wakeman S. Bodie as a "Tin-man". Sarah Bodey joined the First Baptist Church in March of 1843. The 1844 through 1849 Pougkeepsie Village directories list him as Waterman S. Bodey or Waterman S. Body. Subsequent village and city directories list Sarah as either Mrs. Waterman Bodey or Mrs. Wakeman Bodey. She was first listed as a widow in 1862 as Sarah Bodie. Between 1891 and 1893, she was listed as Sarah Bodie in the Old Ladies Home. The *Poughkeepsie Daily Eagle News* reported that Sarah Body died on March 22nd, 1893, in the Old Ladies Home, and recalled the story of her husband 40 years prior and how "Body's Mining Camp to this day bears that name".

In 1848, Bodey tried his luck in New York State politics. He tried running for New York Supreme Court Justice, and received one vote from Dutchess County. After losing by a wide margin, he ran for N.Y. Canal Commissioner and received fourteen votes.

While in El Doraldo County, California, W. S. Bodey had trouble with his debts. In 1854, the year that Hangtown was renamed to Placerville, the local newspaper, the *Mountain Democrat* ran a notice:

> "State of California. County of El Dorado, SS. Cosumnes Township.
> The People of the State of California to W. S. Bodey, Greetings:
> YOU are hereby summoned to be and appear before the undersigned, an acting Justice of the Peace in and for the said county and township, on the 24th day of November next, at 10 o'clock A. M., at my office in Indian Diggings, in said township, to answer the complaint of E. H. Perry and A. T. Lee, who sue to recover the sum of one hundred and sixty-eight dollars upon a due bill of date April 21st, 1854: hereof fail not so to appear and answer, or judgement will be rendered against you by default, for the aforesaid amount, besides costs and damages. Witness my hand, this the 14th day of August, A. D. 1854.   JNO. S. FARISH, J. P."

Wakeman and Sarah kept in contact through letters. Sarah could not read, according to the 1870 census, which listed her as "Sarah Dodey", living in Newark, New Jersey, along with her son Ogden, a tinman who also could not read. The October 9th, 1854, *Sacramento Daily Union* shows two letters waiting for W. S. Bodey at the post office. Sarah apparently used the spelling "Bodey" while Wakeman used "Body" fairly consistently. Wakeman also spent time around Sonora in Tuolumne County. A deed from W. S. Body to Sarah Body was recorded in Sonora on November 13th, 1856 for a one sixth part of a quartz claim (Piatt, website) on "what is commonly known as Old Lonely Hill" . W. S. Bodey's prospecting luck apparently improved a few months before his demise in Mono County, as reported by the August 30th, 1859 *Sacramento Daily Union*:

> "Rich Diggings in Tuolumne. —The richest claim that has been struck in Tuolumne, says the Sonora Democrat, is that of Bodey & Co., at Marlow Diggings. Two "chispas" —one weighing ten ounces five dollars, and the other nine ounces fourteen dollars—were found, one day week before last; and the company took out, in two days' washing, over $1,200."

On December 23rd, 1911, the *Poughkeepsie Daily Eagle News* ran an article about the dilapidated state of the Old Baptist Burying Ground in Poughkeepsie. The cemetery was full of refuse, the fence was broken, large saplings filled the graveyard, stones were broken or missing, and a nearby stable was dumping manure in the graveyard. The article included tombstone inscriptions that were recorded by Dr. J. Wilson Poucher and Miss

Helen W. Reynolds. Among them were four of Bodey's children:

"In memory of William A. O. Bodey, who died Dec. 11, 1852, aged 9 years, 1 month, 12 da. Also, Philip A. Bodey, who died March 15, 1841, aged 1 yr., 10 mo. and 17 da."
"In memory of George A. Bodey, who died March 15th. 1860 aged 19 yr., 1 mo., 1 day."
"Ogden E. Bodey, Co. G 150th. N.Y. Vets. died Jan. 2 .1871. aged 25. (G. A. R. marker.)"

Ogden had enlisted in the Union Army (Grand Army of the Republic) at the age of 16 as a musician. He served as a drummer in the 150th infantry regiment, which fought in the Battle of Gettysburg, and Sherman's March to the Sea. His military pension was provided to his mother. A 1927 *Poughkeepsie Eagle News* article, stated that the cemetery was in the same sorry state, and was being sold to the city to build a school. The bodies were left in place and the stones were moved to the Rural Cemetery in Poughkeepsie.

A funeral was held for W. S. Bodey on November 2nd, 1879, under the auspices of the Pacific Coast Pioneers of Bodie. An eloquent eulogy was presented by the Hon. R. D. Ferguson, Speaker of the Assembly of the State of Nevada and Pioneer member. In his eulogy, he appealed for an enduring monument of granite to be made to "kiss the first golden rays of the coming sun", and have the simple inscription of "BODEY". Bodey was buried in the Masonic Cemetery. After several years of fund-raising and building the monument, President Garfield was assassinated, and the completed monument was used to honor Garfield, while W. S. Bodey's grave became unmarked and forgotten. Bodey's knife was presented to the Pacific Coast Pioneers by Terrence Brodigan, the organizer of the original four prospectors which included Bodey. The May 5th, 1885, *Daily Alta California* reported that the Pacific Coast Pioneers presented Bodey's heavily rusted fifteen inch long Bowie knife to Secretary Ray of the California Museum Association. Shortly afterwards, the association became the Crocker Museum of Art. Unfortunately, the Crocker Museum of Art is unable to locate the knife in their collection, and it is unknown where the knife is presently located.

President Garfield Monument

Terrence Brodigan

Terrence Brodigan is known as the person who led the group, including W. S. Bodey, that first discovered gold in what would become the town of Bodie. Terrence was born in Drogheda, Ireland in 1822. At the age of nineteen, he sailed to New South Wales, Australia, under the bounty program, which paid the immigration costs by an employer. He was listed as a farm laborer, his older brother John a shepherd, and twenty year old sister Hannah, "travelling under the protection of her two brothers", a dairymaid.

The 1860 United States Census shows that children Elizabeth A. and Terrence J. were born in New Zealand about 1848 and 1850, but subsequent census list Elizabeth as being born in Australia, and Terrence being born in California at various later dates. At around 1851, Terrence settled in Sonora, California, with his wife Ann, who was also born in Ireland. He was successful in finding gold on his property in Sonora. In 1856, he built the Sonora Hotel, a large two story building built of slate rock, and a livery stable. He supplied packers over Sonora Pass when rich mineral deposits were found in the Eastern Sierra. In the fall of 1859, he met with the W. S. Bodey party, also from Sonora, in the "Mono Diggins" area, joined forces, and found gold in Bodie.

In 1870, his son George, who became Secretary of State of Nevada, was born. His daughter Elizabeth married John Sanborn, who struck a rich claim in 1859 worth several hundred thousand dollars. In 1877, the Sonora Hotel burnt down, at a loss of $14,600 with $5,500 covered by insurance.

Terrence moved to Bodie and bought up the water rights to springs for supplying good drinking water to businesses in Bodie. He had the water delivered by wagon and charged a dollar a barrel. Good drinking water was not available in Bodie as the local wells were unfit for use due to pollution from slop dumped in the streets by the saloons and restaurants (Piatt 120). The Bodie Water Company had non-potable water flowing from the mines into a reservoir for fire protection. In 1882, Terrence piped water to his subscribers as an article in the November 26th, *Daily Free Press* titled "Fresh Spring Water" reported:

Wooden Pipe - Bodie Museum

"The ditches which are now being run over town are for the purpose of receiving the pipe of T. Brodigan, who is determined to afford all the facilities to purchasers of water that can be furnished by anyone. Mr. Brodigan has been a long time in the business in Bodie, and he feels confident that in view of the fact that his dealings have always been fair and upright, that he certainly retain all his former customers. The pipe will be laid all over town in the next day or so."

He sold his water rights in 1882 to the Pearson Brothers, who used the spring water to make soda water which was bottled in Bodie (Wedertz 18). Bodie's water supply problems were finally solved when water was piped to Bodie from the headwaters of Rough Creek on the eastern slope of Potato Peak about four miles away. Today the same water source is used to to fill a 50,000 gallon underground tank, and the old reservoir is used for overlow.

Terrence died on October 30th, 1896, in his daughter Elizabeth Sanborn's home in Fruitvale, California, at the age of 72, leaving six children, a widow, and a small fortune. Four of his children were still living in Bodie at the time. Curiously, his obituaries mentioned his Bodie water business, but did not mention his role in the discovery of gold in Bodie. The *Oakland Tribune* reported that he was one of the early discoverers of the Comstock lode, and was "at one time the partner of Flood, Fair, Mackay, and other moneyed kings on the Comstock". The *San Francisco Chronicle* reported that "Flood, McKay, and Fair laid up untold wealth after Brodigan had established them in the mining business, but as fast as Brodigan himself had acquired a fortune he would drop it in some deal." The *San Francisco Call* reported:

> "He went to Nevada in 1859 and purchased the whole of Gold Hill for about $500. He furnished the greater part of the capital for the development of the Comstock lode when it was discovered, and was one of the largest owners in the mines. The late James G. Fair, the multimillionaire, was in his employ at one time."

Bodie Overflow Reservoir

James Stuart Cain

James Stuart Cain acquired almost all of the property in Bodie, which made it possible for his family to negotiate the establishment of Bodie as a California State Park. James was born near Rockburn, Quebec. According to his 1855, Russelltown Congregation baptismal record, James was born on April 17th, 1853, "given of the marriage of David Cain and Jennet Stuart". The 1871 Census of Canada shows David and Jennet Cain working on a farm in the Hinchinbrooke subdistrict of Huntingdon, Quebec, with seven children: Isaac 20, James S. 17, Elizabeth 16, Catherine 15, Ellen 13, Euphemia 11, and Jemima 9. David was born in Quebec and was of Irish origin, while Jennet was born in Scotland. In 1874, J. S. Cain immigrated to the United States. He worked in the lumber business in Carson City, Nevada, and moved to Bodie in 1879, after marrying Martha Delilah Wells. Together they had four children. In 1900 their ages were Victor (David) 19, Delilah (Dolly) 18, James 13, and Stuart 18.

Bank Ruins

J. S. Cain went into business freighting lumber across Mono Lake to Bodie, and prospecting various mining claims. By 1888, he was paying Mono County taxes on the Spaulding Patented Mining Claim, 8 lots in the town of Bodie, improvements consisting of 3 houses and an office, Watch $50, Furniture $150, Firearms $20, Sewing Machine $20, Fixtures $150, 3 Wagons $100, Harness $10, Cow $20, Calf $10, Dog $5, Bicycle $25, Money on Hand $3,000, and Unsecured Credits $800. In 1888, he bought a half interest in the Bank of Bodie, and later bought the other half.

By 1906, he owned the Flagstaff and Midnight mining claims. Years later, The Midnight Mine was encroached on by the Standard, and J. S. Cain with attorney William Metson filed suit. The March 6th, 1915, *Chronicle-Union of Bridgeport* reported:

> "The Standard Consolidated Mining Co. that has kept Bodie on the map for so many years was sold the 22nd of Feb. to J. S. Cain Co. of Bodie. Mr. Cain had a suit against the Standard Company for $700,000 for ore taken from the Midnight claim and in the settlement of the suit he got property for consideration of $25,000 and drop the suit."

After buying all of the Standard property, he leased out mining claims for a percentage of the gross, and charged for milling. He continued buying property while living in Bodie. He moved to San Francisco some time after the 1932 fire. J. S. Cain was a big Bodie booster and a spokesperson for the town. The 1930, December 8th, edition of the *Oakland Tribune* reported on one of J. S. Cain's upcoming presentations:

J. S. Cain House

"...incidentally, Bodie, once a busy town of 20,000 people, then a "ghost town", and Jim Cain, who will be the Bodie speaker and town's banker, who bought buildings at 59 cents to $3 a building (the latter was for the huge Miner's Hall) is now reported to be receiving $1999 a month in rentals alone."

The population stated, even if halved, is considered to be quite an exaggeration. According to his obituary in the *Reno Evening Gazette*, J. S. Cain died in Berkeley on October 28th, 1938, at the age of eighty-seven.

One of the amusing stories regarding J. S. Cain is the robbing of the Bodie Bank. The September 2nd, 1916, issue of the *Reno Evening Gazette* reported:

"Dynamite Vault and Secure About $5000 in Cash and Bullion; Came in Machine
BODIE, Cal, Sept. 2.—Four men, traveling in a Maxwell car, one of whom is believed to be from Reno, dynamited the vault of the bank of J. S. Cain & Co., at this place last night securing several thousand dollars in cash, a large quantity of bullion, several hundred dollars worth of jewelry and after rifling the store in which the bank is located, fled into the mountains. In all it is believed that the loss will aggregate from $5000 to $6000, although definite figures have not been given out at this time. The men suspected came to Bodie in an automobile and all four together with their machine were gone this morning when the robbery was discovered. A posse was immediately formed and was sent in all directions to head them off. It is believed they are headed toward Reno, although so far no valuable clue to their present movements has been discovered. First reports placed the loss in cash at $1,000, but later statements were to the effect that it would be less, bullion to the value of $1500 is known, to have been taken. The store of J. S. Cain & Co., was also rifled, a number of revolvers being taken."

Bank Safe

The more conservative *Bridgeport Chronicle-Union* reported a different version of the story. It reported that the robbers came in the bank opening a window in back of the building. The locks on vault, and safe were drilled and a punch driven thru, breaking the tumblers and allowing bolts to be thrown and doors opened. The bank robbers were never found.

Emil Billeb, who wrote the book *Mining Camp Days*, was the superintendent of a Mono Lake lumber company. He married Dolly Cain in 1911, and negotiated the transfer of Bodie to the State of California on behalf of the Cain family.

Ella Cain, who wrote the book *The Story of Bodie*, from which many of the stories of Bodie originated, married David Victor Cain in 1904. She started the book in the 1930's and published it in 1956. She taught at the Bodie School in the early 1900's. Ella started the Bodie Museum in the Miner's Union Hall in the 1950's. In the 1920's, she began collecting Native American baskets. A 1929 Paiute basket originally collected by Ella Cain sold for at record price of $336,250 at a 2005 Bonhams & Butterfields Native American art auction in San Francisco.

Bodie School

GEORGE B. HINKLE

George B. Hinkle was the first Methodist minister in Bodie. He was born on Christmas Day, 1829, in Pleasant Grove, Maryland, along with his twin sister, Elizabeth. He moved to Missouri in 1851 and in 1853 crossed the plains and mountains, following the gold rush to California, where he worked in mining. In 1857, Rev. George Hinkle organized the Methodist Episcopal Church of Dutch Flat, California. In 1860, he was admitted to the California Conference of the Methodist Episcopal Church. His first assignment was in the Mount Shasta District. G. B. Hinkle was described as being very tall. He was not a scholar, nor was he widely read. He did not attend college. However, he had the discipline and training required to be the quintessential itinerant minister, covering circuits by foot with dozens of miles between locations to preach.

In 1869, he married Priscilla Brown, who was born October 10th, 1829, in Pittsburgh, Pennsylvania. They had one son, George, and several grandchildren. The minutes of the 1913 California Annual Conference of the Methodist Episcopal Church included these poignant words in Priscilla's obituary:

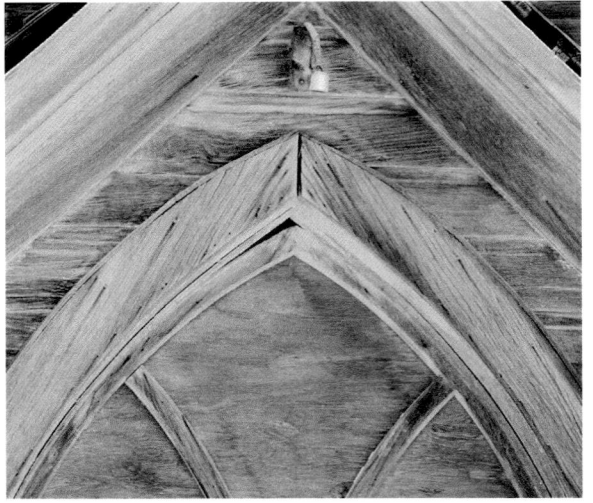

Church Detail

"After her marriage to Mr. Hinkle, she took up the work of an itinerant's wife gladly and never complained at the hardships of a frontier ministry. Many a time they have lived in a tent, until they could get to work and build a house in which to live. In moving long distances, from one charge to another, they have more than once slept out on the desert, for in those days there were no railroads and often no stages, and so they had to move with their own team and camp out where night over took them. She often denied herself of new clothes, a new hat, and the luxuries of living that they might put money into a parsonage or church, or perhaps send it away to help a more needy brother."

G. B. Hinkle spent thirty years in California and Nevada covering such areas as Tuscarora, Elko, Bridgeport, Quincy, Coleville, Winnemucca, Genoa, and Bodie. He had established churches, often times quarrying the rock for the foundations and shaping the timbers with his own hands. In the late 1870's, Reverend Hinkle was assigned the city of Bodie. The 1880 Census shows him living in Bodie. He would preach in private homes, the I.O.O.F. Building, or the Miner's Union Hall. There were no churches in Bodie until 1882. Reverend Hinkle laid the plans for the Methodist Church in Bodie. A group of the congregation who called themselves "The Hinkle Ladies" helped raise the funds to build the church.

In 1880, G. B. Hinkle was assigned the town of Bridgeport and was made Presiding Elder of the Southern District. He preached his last sermon in Reno, Nevada, in 1897 and died in Sacramento, California, on July 7th, 1913. His twin sister died four days earlier. Priscilla died on February 15th, 1914.

Methodist Church

Francis M. Warrington

Francis M. Warrington was the minister in Bodie when the Methodist Church was built. He was assigned to Bodie from 1880 to 1882.

F. M. Warrington was born in Kentucky in 1850. The 1870 United States Census shows Mr. Warrington working as a farm hand in New Salem, Illinois. He graduated from Northwestern University in liberal arts and from Boston University School of Theology. After joining the Illinois Conference in 1875, he transferred to Minnesota and then to Winnamucca, Nevada in 1879, and Bodie in 1880.

He is often quoted from a letter written in January, 1881, in response to an inquiry from Mrs. Thomas D. Penfield about her son in Bodie, in which he states "I do not wonder that you tremble when you think of his surroundings, *a sea of sin, lashed by the tempest of lust and passion.*" He then proceeded to list the events that occurred in Bodie the previous week, which included a shooting and a lynching. Lucinda Penfield from Camden, New York, was inquiring about her only son, twenty-four year old Israel Stoddard Penfield, who travelled in the west during 1879-1882. The full text of the letter as well as a photograph of Stoddard in front of a stage coach can be found in the book. *The Ghost Town of Bodie A California State Park* (Johnson 101).

Methodist Church Interior

His father, Thomas Demilt Penfield, was a successful miller and a partner in the Penfield & Stone firm. He was a prominent citizen and active in Democratic politics. Thomas served as justice of the peace, school commissioner, supervisor, and assemblyman. He was active in the Methodist Episcopal Church and for more than 25 years was chairman of the board of trustees.

After his father's death in 1898, Israel Stoddard Penfield assumed his father's interest in the firm. Israel was a collector of antique furniture. The "Penfield Chair," a chair with the ability to adjust the pitch of the back, was a reproduction from his collection. He never married and lived until he was 88 years old (Penfield 116).

In 1887, F. M. Warrington was transferred to Southern California, where he served until 1906. On May 1st, 1890, at the age of forty, he married twenty-five year old Fanny Lebus, his parishioner who had come to Southern California because of poor health. Fanny was born in Kentucky, and graduated from Cincinnati Wesleyan College. They had a son, Vernon Lebus, who died very young. Fanny died from her long illness on March 2nd, 1893. F. M. Warrington died on January 6th, 1931. His obituary stated that he "suffered almost all his adult life from ill health which made very difficult the performance of his duties as a pastor." His brother, L. P. Warrington, was also a pastor.

Graveyard Fence

E. J. CLINTON

Edmond J. Clinton held the last service at the Methodist Church at Bodie in 1932. He restored the church using his own funds, and held services there. He was born on June 15th, 1872, in Nevada, Missouri. His father, David H. Clinton, started a restaurant in Los Angeles. When working as an officer of the Salvation Army in San Bernardino, Edmond met and married Gertrude Hall on November 2nd, 1895, in Los Angeles. They settled in San Francisco and established the Dennet's Cafeteria chain. They both went to the China mission fields in 1905 as independents. After the 1906 earthquake, they returned to repair damage to their businesses. In 1910 they went to China again for several years. Gertrude Clinton died in 1915 due to complications of delivering their tenth child, Joseph.

In 1919, E. J. Clinton married Rose Potter Crist. Together they followed a "gold-lust dream" to Bodie in 1928 after selling out the restaurant interests to his family. They lived in the Hoover House for a short time before remodeling the Bodie & Benton Railroad Depot as their home. Remodeling included installing indoor plumbing, and using the water tower as the water source. Several of E. J. Clinton's children, including Joseph also lived there. The old railroad depot and water tower can be seen from the town at the top of the hill facing East.

Railroad Depot and Water Tower

E. J. Clinton and W. B. West formed the Clinton-West Corporation. Billy West had been investigating and experimenting with extracting ore from the tailings and surface debris from the Standard mine for ten years. He interested E. J. Clinton in building a mill in 1928 at the cost of $75,000. The plant was designed to process 500 tons of ore every 24 hours. It was expected that each ton processed would extract gold worth $3.50. The "dry land dredger", powered by two 150 horsepower motors, was built on a forty by forty foot steel I-beam frame mounted on rollers. There was a ninety foot dragline with a bucket capable of operating for a distance of six hundred feet from the mill. The mill was complete by the end of November, but operation had to be suspended due to the deep snow. A photograph of the bizarre looking "metallurgical monstrosity" can be found in the book *Bodie "The Mines Are Looking Well..."* (Piatt 255).

In 1929, it was decided to use the flotation process to separate gold from the ore using large cyanide leaching tanks to extract enough gold to make the operation profitable. Ore was shipped to the Lucky Boy operation in Hawthorne, Nevada for testing. It was found that with the flotation process, 95% of the value instead of 65% of the value could be obtained. By the end of the year it was reported that the operation was processing 400 tons daily with good savings. The mill feed was from the dumps, and a large trench dug under the dumps which included a rich strata of ore. By the Summer of 1930, the Clinton-West Corporation ran out of money, and sold its interest to the Treadwell Yukon Company. E. J. Clinton went back to the restaurant business, working for his son, Clifford.

Moonrise

Thomas Miller

Thomas Miller worked as a teamster in Bodie. He was born in Canada on August 4th, 1859, and immigrated in 1878. He and Jennie Wittman of Bodie were married in Lyon county, Nevada, in 1887, and three years later had a son, Thomas G. Miller. Jennie left her husband and son because of a troubled marriage. She stayed with friends and her sister, Mrs. Hansen, in San Francisco. On July 19th, 1894, Jennie committed suicide. Four days later, an article appeared in the San Francisco Chronicle, titled "SUICIDES OF WOMEN", which was an exposé of how records were suppressed for women who committed suicide in order to protect family privacy:

"Thomas Miller, the husband of the deceased is to arrive today from Bodie, where he is a teamster and contractor. Mrs. Miller, who was 24 years old was married seven or eight years ago. The couple had one child, a boy now about 4 years old. Mrs. Miller came to this city from Bodie two or three months ago, Mrs. Hanson said, and until two weeks ago stopped with a friend, Mrs. Agnes Holt, on Scott street, near California. She then went to her sister's home. Her purpose when coming to San Francisco was to leave her husband, and she had a suit for divorce instituted. Lately she longed intensely for her little boy, and her sister persuaded her to abandon the divorce suit and agree to return home. On July 13th, she sent a telegram to her husband saying that the divorce suit would be dismissed and that she and Mrs. Hansen would start for Bodie in a few days. She told him to answer by telegraph. No answer arrived. The next day she wrote Mr. Miller a letter. A telegram received by Mr. Hansen last Friday, the day after her death, stated that the husband received the letter of the 14th on the 20th. Mrs. Miller brooded over the absence of a response from her husband and it is thought that the feeling thus caused influenced her to end her life.

Had Mrs. Miller lived she would have celebrated her twenty-fourth birthday last Friday. Her mother lives in Alameda. Her maiden name was Witman. Deputy Jones, in beginning his explanation, first spoke

Miller Table and Chairs

Miller House Kitchen

in such a way as to suggest that he kept the news from the public so that Mrs. Hansen might not be tempted to commit suicide also. A glance at Mrs. Hansen yesterday showed that she is a lady with self-control, She said "Jennie and I were getting ready to go out and have her lawyer stop the divorce case. She had packed her trunk on Wednesday, and she and I were going to Bodie next Monday. I went to my room to get a cloak, and she stepped into another room to put on a coat. I heard shooting. It sounded like the pop of firecrackers. I threw up the front window and looked down the street. Seeing nothing there, I went into the hall. Smoke was coming through the window of my sister's room into the hallway, and I thought she might have been shooting to scare me, but I dreaded to go in. I feared that if I did and saw her dead or wounded, I would give way. I did not want to attract the attention of people in front of the house or in the employment office, where there is usually a big crowd. So I kept myself from screaming or fainting, and went down stairs to the office. I spoke to the clerk there, saying I thought my sister had shot herself, and I wanted him to go to the room and see. I saw Dr. Quinlan crossing the street and sent an errand boy after him. He went into the room when I said 'I think my sister Jennie has shot herself.' She had not answered when I called to her. I was still afraid to go into the room. He said when he came out that she had died instantaneously."

Miller House Bedroom

Thomas went back to Bodie. Tax records in 1893 indicate Thomas owned a house on Green Street, stables for his five American Horses, a twenty-five dollar watch, furniture worth forty dollars, two wagons, harness, a dozen chickens, a sewing machine, and a dog.

On October 13th, 1897, thirty-seven year old Thomas married twenty year old Jessie Christiana Currie. Together they had a daughter, Laura, and a son, James. Thomas died at the age of forty-four on December 17th, 1903 and is buried in Bodie. Jessie moved to Inyo County, where she worked as a tax collector. She often visited Bodie. In July of 1911, she gave a Saturday night party at the Miner's Union Hall, for young Thomas Miller's twenty-first birthday. There was a large crowd with dancing and feasting.

Jessie had a number of relatives living in the area. Her father, Charles H. Currie, was born in Scotland and married Anna M. Young in Minnesota. In 1885, the family moved to Mono Lake, and a little later came to Bishop. One of Jessie's sisters was Annie Miller, who operated the Occidental Hotel, and after it burned down, a boarding house on Green Street. Annie was married to William Miller, Thomas's brother.
Another of Jessie's sisters, Margaret Calhoun, wrote a book about the Curtis family and other early settlers in the area titled Pioneers of Mono Basin. In 1921, J. S. Cain bought the Miller House from Jessie Miller.

Miller House Doorway

HARVEY BOONE

Harvey Boone was the proprietor of the general store in downtown Bodie at the intersection of Main and Green Streets. He was born in Pennsylvania on December 6th, 1832. It is often stated that Harvey Boone was a direct descendant of Daniel Boone. The relationship is more accurately described as first cousins thrice removed. Daniel Boone's grandfather, George Boone III, who was born in 1666 in Devonshire, England, and died on February 27th, 1744, in Berks County Pennsylvania, was Harvey Boone's great great great grandfather. The following shows the two family paternal branches with birth dates:

George Boone III 1666

1696	Squire Boone	William Boone	1724
1734	Daniel Boone	George Boone	1690
		Hezekia Boone	1764
		George Boone	1794
		Harvey Boone	1832

Harvey married his first wife, Julia E. Hayden, in St. Louis, Missouri, on the 4th of July, 1876. They had three children, Harvey Jr., Alice, and Julia. In 1881, shortly after the birth of Julia, her mother, 38 years old, died and was buried in Bodie. In 1889, Harvey married Ada Adele Kinney Stewart, and together with Harvey had two children, Stanley and Leslie.

In 1878, Harvey recorded a hay, grain, and grocery partnership in Bodie with William H. Dolman, who lived in Treasure City, Nevada, around 1870, as did Harvey. The partnership was short lived.

A year later, Harvey recorded a partnership with Jas. W. Wright, who was a P. G. (Past Grand) of the I.O.O.F. in Goldfield, Nevada, and in 1871, started a new chapter in Pioche, Nevada, where Harvey became a member, and later was the treasurer of the I.O.O.F. in Bodie

Boone & Wright Store Window

Boone & Wright General Store

for many years. Together they operated the Boone and Wright general store. Harvey was active in Republican politics, was a convention delegate, county supervisor, school trustee, Bodie Water Company president, and the postmaster of nearby Masonic, where he established another general store. He and his family moved to Masonic in 1905.

In 1885, Harvey Boone paid Mono County taxes on his store and warehouse, stables, dwelling, two houses, Gilson's old store and tin shop, stock of groceries, provisions, and hardware worth $10,000, store fixtures, five wagons, harness, robes, four American horses, six half-bred horses, two dozen poultry, five tons of barley, and twenty tons of hay. Ada Boone paid taxes on a cattle ranch in Bridgeport, with house and barn, machinery, hogs, cattle, and about 50 horses. Several large freight teams were leased out. From the *Chronicle-Union:*

May 12, 1897-
"FREIGHTING.—Hunt's team arrived from Carson on Tuesday with freight for this town, and on Monday Boone's two big teams, 14 horses each, arrived with freight for Harvey Boone, of Bodie."

November 28. 1901-
"Chas. Frey left yesterday for Sodaville with Mrs. Boone's 12-horse team, intending to freight between that place and Tonopah."

Ada sold the cattle ranch to the Conways in 1902. Harvey Boone died in Santa Clara, California, on January 30th, 1917, and Ada died in Bridgeport on December 2nd, 1937.

In later years, a Shell service station was added, The general store, named the Bodie Mercantile Store, was operated by S. W. Cain and W. B. Evans, who also operated the Bridgeport Store and Garage.

Path to Boone & Wright Store

Boone Feed and Tack Room

Bodie Garage

Shell Service Station

Eli Johl

Eli Johl is known as the simple butcher of Bodie who married Lottie Johl, the "soiled dove" who attempted to become respectable, but was shunned by the town, and died of accidental poisoning. Research reveals a fascinating and compelling glimpse into their lives.

Elias Johl was born on July 14th, 1842, in the village of Rust, near Baden-Baden, Germany. He had thirteen brothers and sisters. His oldest brother, Abraham, immigrated to the United States, and became a merchant in Arkansas just before the American Civil War. He served in the Confederate Army as a private, and later moved to Memphis, Tennessee. Eli's father, Hirsch Johl, was a shopkeeper. Following Hirsch's death in 1864, a number of other family members emigrated from Germany early in January, 1865. Eli came several months later, arriving in New York on March 29th, 1865. While most of his relatives settled in the South, Eli struck out to the West to seek his fortune.

By 1870, Eli was in Nevada working as a butcher in Mineral Hill, which sprang up after rich silver deposits were discovered in 1869. The town grew to four hundred people, but became a ghost town after it burnt down in 1872 and was mined out by 1873. Eli lost $1,800 worth of property in the first of a number of fires that would plague him. In February. 1876, he was appointed as a postmaster of the town of Lida, Nevada, where his friend, Clem Ogg and partners hauled out 45,000 feet of lumber. Clem Ogg, who was elected sheriff of Esmeralda County in 1878, was described as large prickly bearded man with long unkempt hair. He was a bullwacker who drove teams of oxen and was said to be diabolically accurate in wielding a twenty foot long bullwhip with a three foot handle (Wilson 122).

By 1877, Eli moved to the towns of Belleville and Candelaria, which are about 75 miles east of Bodie. Silver was discovered near Candelaria in 1863. A 20-stamp mill was built in Belleville about 8 miles west of the mines to process the ore because of the shortage of water in Candelaria. Water had to be packed in from Belleville, a town of 300 people, to Candelaria, a town of 750 people. All are now ghost towns. In 1880, advertisements in the Candelaria newspaper, *The True Fissure*, indicate that Eli Johl and John Goodwin were proprietors of the Candelaria Market, a meat market on Main Street in Candelaria. Eli was also a proprietor, along with Sheriff Clem Ogg of the Belleville Hotel on Main Street in Belleville. The Belleville Hotel had a large ballroom and elegant connecting bar, where large Christmas, New Years Eve, and Fourth of July parties were held. On May 21st, 1881, an article in *The True Fissure*, titled "Eli Johl's Big Prospect" revealed that Eli was successful in prospecting for silver:

> "Eli Johl, the well known butcher, is a constant prospector: that is he has men all year around out in the hills prospecting. One day this week a valuable find was made in one of these locations. It is about eighteen miles from Belleville, and Mr. Johl says that the only difficulty is the lack of water. The ore, at a few feet from the surface shows astonishing assays: going away up in the hundreds."

Eli dissolved his partnership in the Candelaria Market, and within two months married Lottie Calhoun. The marriage was conducted on the Fourth of July, 1881, by Eli's friend and boarder, A. G. Turner, Justice of the

Johl House - Bodie

Peace, and witnessed by Sheriff Clem Ogg and Mrs. John Ellis, Lottie's friend who as Hattie Clark had married four months prior. The marriage was recorded several days later with the name Ely Johl, which Eli used on a number of documents. Eli and Lottie had a wedding celebration lasting several days as described by the July 9th, 1881, edition of *The True Fissure* titled "In Hymen's Bond":

> "Last Monday evening at Belleville, Eli Johl and Miss Lottie Calhoun were joined in the bonds of wedlock. A large number of personnel friends of the high contracting parties were present, and after the ceremony wine flowed like water. The bride was elegantly and tastefully dressed in a lavender silk, trimmed with bands of velvet of a darker shade, fringe of balls and tassels, and the whole finished and enriched by light corn-colored lace. The toilette was extremely rich and becoming. The bridegroom wore the usual regulation black with white vest. A feature of the festivities was the visit, at a late hour, of ten or a dozen masquers who added much to the hilarity of the occasion by their antics. At a late hour the company withdrew, but on the following day and evening the festivities were renewed, the many friends of the newly wedded couple vieing with each other in having a good time."

The masqueres included Clem Ogg, who wore "a pink tarleton cut bias on the off side; hair done up in the wash room of the Belleville Hotel." Dan McDonald wore "an Elizabethan of quilted cherry; hair done in firkin butter." William Moraghan wore a "Martha Washington costume of drab silk, overlaid with point lace; tansy and geranium leaves in hair, done up trimmed with harness buckles."

Lottie Calhoun was born in 1853, as Charlotte J. Wilson in Keosauqua, Iowa. Van Buren County Genealogical Society and census records indicate that Lottie's mother, Nancy Ann Swearengen, born on Christmas Eve, 1829, married George W. Wilson in 1849. They had two daughters, Mary and Charlotte, and lived on a farm in Farmington, Iowa. In 1856, Nancy was remarried to Henry C. Houk, who was killed in the battle of Fort Donelson in the civil war. In 1872, she married Daniel Faron. In 1913, Nancy, a life long Methodist, died at the age of 84. She had lived most of her life in Keosauqua. Her obituary did not mention her first marriage or first two daughters.

On December 12th, 1868, a marriage license was recorded for Charlotte Wilson and Newton Robert Calhoun in Van Buren County. However, the certificate part of the recording was never completed within the ninety days required. It is possible they were never legally married. They lived on a farm that Newton bought from his parents in 1867. On April 22nd, 1870, their daughter Mattie was born. A year later, Newton Robert and Charlotte J. Calhoun sold the farm to Newton's older brother. In 1876, Newton, Lottie, and Mattie moved to Calaveras County, California. They were separated a year later. It remains a mystery why Lottie and Newton split up, or how Lottie got her reputation as a prostitute.

Lottie Johl - Bodie Museum

The 1880 census does show a Lottie Roberts living in Candelaria with Lulu Gorden, who ran the Lulu Gorden Dance Hall, which was about a block away from the Candelaria Meat Market (Shamberger 48). Perhaps this was her. She had moved to Candelaria from Reno, where she advertised in the *Reno Evening Gazette* a

Saturday night "Social Dance" at her home on Lincoln Avenue. When she moved her landlord filed a complaint against her for stealing bed sheets. She was referred to as "Naughty Lottie" in a November 8th, 1879, *Reno Evening Gazette* article. Lottie was robbed by Charles Gray, referred to as "Wicked Charles" of $1,520 worth of money and jewelry. Charles Gray was arrested several years later in Bodie for battery of "a lady well known in Bodie" when she demanded payment for breaking her jewelry (McGrath 156).

Following the wedding, Eli and Lottie lived in a house in back of the Belleville Hotel. Eli was a partner with J. C. McDonald for most of his mining claims. In 1881, before the wedding, they recorded claims in the Garfield Mining District for the Delaware No. 1, 2, and 3 mines, the Vermont 1, 2, and 3 mines, and the General Garfield mine. Another mining claim, the Lottie, was also recorded at this time. According to the February 13th, 1882, edition of the *Reno Evening Gazette*:

> "Last week assays were made from samples of rock brought from Garfield by James Cross and Mr. Johl. The samples were taken from two different locations and assayed $16,000 and $8,000 per ton, respectively."

Sewing Machine

James Cross was the mill superintendant. Eli and Lottie were married for almost a year when a tragedy occurred as described by the Saturday, June 3rd, 1882, edition of the *True Fissure*:

> "RIDDLED WITH BUCKSHOT.
> Another Fatal Quarrel Between Mining Partners"

"This community had not recovered from the shock of one fatal shooting affair when another occurred. The scene of the second tragedy was at Belleville, and happened about half-past ten o'clock on Thursday morning. The principals were Eli Johl and J. C. McDonald, who have been partners in some of the first discovered and best mines in Garfield district. Bad blood had existed between the two men for some months past, yet it did not come to any demonstration until early in the week. Johl had been to the mine at Garfield district, and about Luning, and all who knew the men looked for a serious meeting at the latter place. Johl took the train on Wednesday evening and returned to his home at Belleville. About one o'clock the next morning McDonald came into the town on horseback, went to Johl's house, made a disturbance with such a purpose that it was evident he intended it to be heard. Finding this did not cause the anticipated resistance, he raised the window of Mr. and Mrs. Johl's bed-room and used some very vile language, which is said to have been more forcible than elegant. This conduct continued at intervals until toward noon, when McDonald made his last visit to the house. What passed between the men at this time is not yet known, but it must have been of a further intimidating nature, and made Johl anxious for his personal safety. Before McDonald had gone seventy-five feet Johl opened fire on him with a double barreled shotgun loaded with buckshot. McDonald was moving across the street, away from the house, and fell dead from the effects of the first and only shot fired."

The article states that Judge Stevens ruled that Eli "was discharged, the evidence proving conclusively that he was justified in what he had done."

Another tragedy occurred three months later. The September 10th, 1882, issue of the *True Fissure* reported that a fire burnt down the Belleville Hotel. The house in back of the hotel where Lottie and Eli lived also burnt down. They were able to save the doors, windows, furniture, and other articles. Sometime after this tragedy they moved to Bodie. In 1883, Eli sold his mules and harness, jennies and pack equipment, wagons, and mining equipment of the Garfield Mining Company. By 1884, he was working for the Union Market in Bodie. In 1886, Lottie's daughter, Mattie, was married in Bodie. An article appeared in the May 6th, 1886, edition of the *Birmingham Enterprise*, a Van Buren County, Iowa, newspaper:

"Married. -- At the residence of the bride's mother, Mrs. Eli Johl, in Bodie, Mono County, Cal, April 14 1886 by the Rev. G. B. Hinkle, Wm. C. Toon of Calaveras County, and Miss Mattie Mary Calhoun, of Bodie. Wm. O. Toon is a native of California, and was raised in Calaveras county, where we believe he was born. He is a young man of twenty-two and like most born on that coast, is of great promise. Mrs. Mattie M. Toon was born in Winchester, Van Buren County, Iowa; her mother, Mrs. Eli Johl, having been born at Keosauqua and was formerly Mrs. N. R. Calhoun, of Winchester, Iowa. They are descended from the Wilsons, who were thirty years ago pioneers in what was then a pioneer country. Mrs. Toon has just attained her sixteenth birthday, and was dressed in white satin, trimmed with cream colored Spanish lace, white illusion veiling trailing the floor, surmounted by a diadem of orange blossoms."

Johl Kitchen

A similar article titled "A BODIE BELLE IS REMOVED FROM OUR MIDST" and subtitled "The Ceremony Takes Place in the Presence of a Large Circle of Friends and Witnesses" appeared in one of the Bodie newspapers:

"Wine of various varieties flowed copiously, in which the bride and groom, hostess and host were toasted liberally. This wedding supper was really a banquet, served with fresh oysters, ice cream and coffee, nine thousand feet above the sea..."

"Congratulations over, music and singing came next in order, in which many guests, the amiable hostess (Mrs. Johl), and the young bride herself took part; the whole tending to enliven the feelings of the large throng..."

Mattie lived to be 103 years old. On her 100th birthday, Mattie Baker recalled her life in the April 24th, 1970, edition of the Hayward, California newspaper, *The Daily Review*, written by Ernestine Wiseman:

"Mrs. Baker was born in Iowa in 1870, the daughter of a Civil War couple. Her parents brought her to California when she was six years old and separated when she was seven. She spent the next nine years being shifted from one relative or foster home to another, until, at 16, her father sent for her to come to Sheep's Ranch in the lusty Mother Lode country. The town's only "proper" amusement establishment was a skating rink and there she met William Toon and agreed to marry him. Her mother, by this time living in the raucous mining town of Bodie - now a historical ghost town monument - invited them to come to her place for the wedding The couple went by stage coach and the "speedy" train, to be greeted by scores of guests. Mrs. Baker's mother also had acquired a degree of wealth and so brought in crabs

Johl House Interior

from San Francisco Bay for the wedding feast. The couple went back to Sheep's Ranch where a daughter, (Mrs. King), was born and a son, James. The latter showed great promise as a musician but was tragically killed in an explosion at 22 years of age, trying to quash a fire at a San Lorenzo powder plant. Mr. Toon died after the couple had been married only 11 years and shortly after her mother passed away in Bodie, the result of an accidental poisoning. Mrs. Baker decided to move to Bodie but life there proved so rigorous she came to Sacramento to open a boarding house."

In 1887, the Johls first began paying personal property taxes in Mono County. Listed were a watch $25, furniture $40, piano $75, and a sewing machine $10. By 1890, taxes were added for a home on the northwest corner of the Post Office. By 1896, a dog $5, piano $450, jewelry $120, furniture $250, and about 8 houses were added. By 1900, several saloons were added. In addition, the Johls owned a number of mining claims, such as the "Little Stringer", for which 20 tons of ore were eventually processed.

On July 28th, 1892, the first of Bodie's great fires burnt down most of the downtown, including the butcher store operated by Charles B. Donnelly and Eli Johl. The reported loss in the fire was $8000 for Eli with $500 covered by insurance, and $1600 for Donnelly. After the fire, Johl and Donnelly recorded a butcher partnership in Mono County. In May, of 1894, Lottie went to San Francisco and sued the Mathias Gray music dealers for insurance on her piano lost in the fire.

The chapter titled "Rivalry Between the Butchers' Wives" in Ella Cain's book, *The Story of Bodie*, told of the competition between Lottie and Annie Donnelly, Charles Donnelly's wife. Their two large oil paintings, which hang side by side in the Bodie Museum, illustrate the rivalry. Ella wrote of the town shunning Lottie because of her past; Lottie gave a party and no one came; the town was shocked when she unmasked at a masquerade ball and was asked to leave. There may have been some truth to these stories, but Ella Cain is known to have taken "artistic license" in a number of her stories. Ella wrote that Annie Donnelly, the nemesis of Lottie, was very upset when Eli married Lottie, but they were married long before they came to Bodie and joined the Donnelly's in business. Eli had joined the A.O.U.W. (Ancient Order of United Workmen), and the Knights of Pythias after Charles Donnelly sponsored him as a member. Eli attended a number of masquerade balls with Lottie along with many of the leading citizens of Bodie. Some newspaper excerpts:

Checkers

"Mrs. Johl was the most richly dressed lady on the floor. The costume attracted attention. Eli Johl, as Prince Carnival, was gorgeously attired-the most richly dressed male character on the floor."
"Eli Johl-appeared as Eli Johl in a black domino. Mrs. Eli Johl -Flower Girl- This ladies costume was very much admired"
"Mrs. Johl, California—a gorgeous, golden glittering costume; Eli Johl, domino"

On November 7th, 1899, Lottie died of poisoning. Dr. Cox signed the death certificate, specifying the cause of accidental poisoning. The Mono County volume *"Inquisition 1887-"*, which recorded coroner's inquests

Johl House Stove

until 1920 cannot be found. If there was an inquest, it would probably would have specified what Lottie had taken. Ella Cain wrote that a mistake was made in filling the prescription, although newspapers of the time did not confirm this as they normally would have. The *Chronicle-Union* reported:

"Sudden Death.—A great gloom was cast over Bodie on Tuesday by the death of Mrs. Eli Johl, a mistake having been made, it is said, in taking a dose of poison instead of salts. Doctors Cox and Robinson did all in their power to save her but without avail."

The town gossip was that Lottie committed suicide. The November 10th, 1899, *Reno Evening Gazette* reported:

"H.G. Schnider of Bodie arrived here last evening en route for Oregon where his mother is seriously ill. Mr. Schnider reports Bodie quiet, the latest sensation being the death of Mrs. E. Jeoul, who committed suicide by poisoning several days ago."

Eli, of course, was devastated. He decorated Lottie's grave with her photograph, flowers and greenery which looked like Christmas trees and wreaths. A photograph of Eli standing by Lottie's decorated grave, with a little snow on the ground, shows a very well dressed, distinguished looking gentleman holding a Hamburg hat in his hand with a plaintive look on his face and a number a children standing by. The photograph can be found in the book "*Images of America Bodie 1859-1962*" (Geissinger 47). A similar photograph, captioned "The Grandest Grave", identifying Eli can be found in the book "*Yesterday's California*" (Leadabrand 58).

Lottie Johl Grave

On March 31st, 1900, the *Chronicle-Union* reported that "Eli Johl and daughter, Mrs. Toon, and child, of Bodie, drove over from Bodie on Thursday to enjoy our balmy spring weather a few days." They probably were settling the estate from Lottie's death. About $2,000 worth of property was still in Lottie's name. On April 18th, Eli petitioned Superior Court for Lottie's property. The petition was granted on April 30th because it was community property. In 1896, Eli recorded a quit claim deed to Lottie of his property, and six months later Lottie recorded a quit claim deed back to Eli. They did a similar legal maneuver in Belleville.

Eli's younger brother, Sol H. Johl, a saloon keeper and coffee dealer in Little Rock, Arkansas, visited Eli in

Johl House Chair

the Spring of 1903. At the end of the year, Eli left for a trip to visit relatives, many who he had not seen for thirty years. Besides visiting Sol, he visited relatives in Memphis Tennessee, Burlington Illinois, Louisville Kentucky, and Greenville Mississippi. He may have visited Illinois a decade earlier, perhaps with Lottie, because the Bodie Museum has a broken red souvenir glass from the 1893 Chicago Worlds Fair with his name engraved on it.

In Greenville, he probably visited his sister in law, Fanny Johl, wife of Abraham. Fanny died in 1905 and was buried in Memphis. A number of Eli's relatives were buried in Memphis during the great yellow fever epidemic of 1878. By March of 1904, Eli was back in Bodie. The April 11th, 1904, *Chronicle-Union* noted:

Johl 1893 World's Fair Glass

"The ladies of Bodie petitioned the Board of Supervisors this week to close the Nickel-in-the-slot machines. The board didn't have the power to comply and so were forced to lay the matter on the table. The officers of the County are looking into the matter and if complaints are made the whole matter of gambling in the county will be stopped."

Two months later, Sheriff Kirkwood arrested Eli and others for operating Nickle-in-the-slot machines. On October 8th, 1904, Eli became one of the proprietors of the Occidental Hotel in Bodie, and obtained a liquor license. On the October 29th, the *Chronicle-Union* reported on Eli's artistic abilities:

"Eli Johl, the decorative artist of the Donnelly Johl Co. meat market, has been showing his skill with the knife this week. He has at the City Market a decorated mutton which has been the subject of much favorable criticism. It has a surprising the number of flowers, vines and scrolls he has been able to trace on the fat carcass. A 700 pound porker has also been on exhibition during the week. The pig must have been fed well one day and starved the next as the flesh shows a streak of lean and a streak of fat."

In 1906, the partnership between Johl, Donnelly, and P. J. Conway was dissolved. Eli sold most of his property to J. S. Cain. Two years later, Eli was in New York City planning a visit to his native Germany. On April 24th, he applied for a passport which specified that Ely Johl, born in Rust, Germany on July 14th, 1842, had lived in Bridgeport, California for 42 years. It stated that he was five foot five inches tall, had blue eyes, grey hair, a low forehead, a proportionate nose, medium mouth, round chin, healthy complexion, and a round face.

In September of 1908, *The Chronicle-Union* ran a number of articles titled "MISSING":

"Eli Johl, formerly of Bodie, is numbered among the missing. He left Bodie over a month ago and nothing has been learned of him after reaching Reno although many inquiries have been made. He was in poor health and it is feared that he has died."

In December, 1909, Eli steamed from Hamburg to Liverpool on a return trip from Germany. The 1910 census shows Ely Johl living at 368 West Sixth Street, Little Rock, Arkansas, and working as a proprietor of a meat market. His younger brother, Sol, was living a few blocks away. It remains unknown where and when Eli died.

In later years, after the 1932 fire, the post office moved to the old Johl house. Perhaps this explains the presence of the eerie portrait of George Washington in the dining room.

Washington Portrait - Lottie Johl House

Annie U. Donnelly

Annie Pagdin is known as the English artist who married Charles B. Donnelly, Eli Johl's partner in the butcher business in Bodie. They were married on November 3rd, 1879, the day after the funeral for W. S. Bodey. She was 26 years old, and her name at the time was Anna Milliken. Charles was 38 and lived in Mono County since at least 1870, where he worked as a dairyman with a small herd of about 17 dairy cows in Bridgeport until he moved to Bodie in 1878. The marriage was reported in the *Bodie Free Press*, and was recorded in beautiful handwriting in the Mono County marriage records by Reverend Hinkle, as Minister of the Gospel:

"Chas. B. Donnelly's Father was a native of Vermont, and his mother Canada. And Anna Milliken parents were natives of England. Anna Milliken was married before to Charles Milliken who is still living. Charles B. Donnelly was born in Point Fortune Canada, and Anna Milliken was born in Chesterfield England."

Hannah Utley Pagden was born on July 11th, 1852. In 1861, she was living in Chesterfield with her widowed mother Elizabeth and older sister Maria. Ella Cain in her book *The Story of Bodie* referred to her as Annie Pagdin, and the PAGDEN grave in Bodie. The PAGDIN name is on the mysterious hollow headstone in the Bodie graveyard with missing epitaph plates. Bodie folklore is that the hollow area in the marker was used to transfer liquor during prohibition. Presumably, Elizabeth, Annie's mother, born in Wentworth, England in 1811, is buried in the grave, although there does not appear to be a Mono County death record.

Pagdin Grave

In 1868, Maria was a member of the Daniel D. McArthur Company, one of the last Mormon pioneer wagon trains to go overland to the Utah territory. Maria took a steamship chartered by Brigham Young from Liverpool to New York, and the railroad to Benton, Wyoming. On August 14th, Maria walked along with a train of 61 oxen drawn wagons and 411 people, arriving in Salt Lake on September 2nd, 1868. A month later, on October 6th, she married William Joseph Goulder in Fillmore, Utah. William emigrated from England, and arrived in Utah with Captain Miller's Company in 1862.

In 1869, Hannah and her mother Elizabeth arrived in Fillmore after riding on the newly completed transcontinental railroad. They were financed by the Perpetual Emigration Fund, which aided impoverished converts to the LDS faith moving west (Ward 208). Elizabeth lived with her daughter Maria and husband, while Hannah worked as a domestic for Matilda and Thomas Rice King. The Kings were prominent Mormon pioneers. Their son William lost his wife during childbirth in 1868. A year later, William was called on his second mission to the island of Oahu. He was counseled by Brigham Young to take another wife while his children stayed with his parents. The book, *Kings of the Kingdom* by Larry R. King describes the King's lives during this time.

Maria died on July, 19th, 1871, at the age of 28 with her maiden name reported in the *Deseret News* as

Mariah Pagdin. By 1872, when Elizabeth Kane, who wrote the book *Twelve Mormon Homes* visited the King family, Hannah apparently was gone because Matilda complained about the lack of help. The Salt Lake City directory of 1874 lists a Miss Annie Pagdin, working as a hairdresser. At some point, Annie married Charles Milliken, and she and her mother moved to Bodie. It remains a mystery what happened to the marriage, and who Charles was. He may have actually been Willis Milliken. On April, 8th, 1879, Willis Milliken in Deer Lodge, Montana Territory, deeded property in Bodie to his wife, Annie Milliken, "for her separate estate especially relinquishing for himself and his heirs in any respect as community property." Willis was a saloon keeper who adverised a saloon called the "Bank Exchange"in Reno. He was also an owner of the Acme Mining Co. in Bodie, which incorperated in March, 1879 with capital of $10,000,000, in shares of $100 each. The 1880 U.S. Census lists 39 year old Willis Milliken living in Bodie with the occupation of "gentleman", born in the "US", and "married" to a 17 year old Annie Milliken born in Denmark. The Donnellys were not listed in the 1880 census.

Ella Cain wrote that Annie supported herself and her mother by giving oil painting lessons and selling paintings. The book *The Ghost Town of Bodie*, by Russ and Anne Johnson, shows a newspaper ad titled "Lessons in Oil Painting", stating that Mrs. Charles B. Donnelly was "prepared to organize a class in oil painting or she will give private lessons." (109)

Annie and Charles attended a number of balls. In November, 1879, Mrs. Charles Donnelly was awarded a handsome jewel casket of solid silver as a waltz prize for which twenty-five couples competed. In March, 1880, Annie attended the second annual Grand Firemen's Ball. It was reported "Mrs. Donnelly as Night, looked somber, but attractive." At another ball it was reported "as she is a very graceful dancer she was much admired and her hand was eagerly sought after by gentleman dancers." In later years, the Donnelly's did not appear in the list of attendees of masquerade balls. Ella Cain described her as being a large, pretentious, and haughty person. Annie was active in the Methodist Church and decorated the church with greens and lilies on Easter. The Donnellys moved to Burlingame, California, where Charles' sister Eva lived, but in 1908 moved back to Bodie after a year because Charles missed his old friends and his "favorite cocktail as compounded by Old Maes" (Anton Maestretti). A July, 1910 *Bridgeport Chronicle-Union* paper reported several society parties that Annie attended.

They moved to Fruitvale (Oakland) in 1911. Annie died in 1915, and Charles in 1918. They are buried in the Mountain View Cemetery in Oakland.

Donnelly House

Sam Leon

Sam Leon was the owner of the Bodie Cafe, which is now called Sam Leon's Bar. Short obituaries in the Reno newspapers stated that Sam Leon was born in China on November 14th, 1879, and died at the age of 75 in Reno on February 20th, 1955, and that he worked in Reno, Bishop, and other cafes in the area. His 1920 census record stated he was born in Honolulu, and 1930 listed California. The book *Corbett Mack The Life of a Northern Paiute*, tells of how Corbett Mack met Sam when buying "moohoo'oo" (opium) in Wabuska, Nevada. Sam was a dope and booze dealer. Corbett says,

> "Already told you about Ah Sam? How he make friend with these Indians? 'Cause Ah Sam, he marry them Indian girl: first wife's name Pozeewa'a; second's Gertie Green, from Fallon...'Cause Ah Sam, he like to gamble with them Indians.... Yes, sir! " (Mack 139)

Pozeewa'a was Daisy Benton's Paiute name. According to the book, Comstock Women: The Making of a Mining Community, Sam Leon, who used the names Wong Leong, Ah Sam, and Sam Wong, married Daisy Benton in 1910 (James 223).

Daisy and Sam had a daughter named Laura, but Daisy died not long after Laura was born. The March 17th, 1915 *Virginia City Daily Territorial Enterprise* ran an article titled "Child Accompanies Father to Prison":

> "A pathetic feature in connection with the case of Sam Leon, the Chinaman sentenced in Carson to nine month's imprisonment following his conviction for disposing of liquor to the Indians, is the fact that he is encumbered with a little two-year-old girl, who insists on staying with "dad". Three years ago the Chinaman was married to a squaw in the Wabuska country and the child is the result of that union. A year ago the mother died and since that time the little one has been the constant companion of the father, and now with the latter in the Washoe county jail the child, young as she is, balks at the idea of separation."

Further articles stated that a Mrs. Kee from Virginia City took charge of Sam's daughter after "the parting created a sad scene", and Laura was sent to a San Francisco missionary school.

The 1920 census shows Sam, married to Gertie, and daughter Laura running a restaurant near Gardnerville, Nevada. Sam also continued travelling all over the area in his Velie automobile plying his trade as a "sagebrush bartender". In March of 1924, Sam Leon was arrested again along with Corbett Mack and five others in the Yerrington Indian Colony because of the deaths of two men fighting over a women during a three day booze and dope festival. Corbett says:

> "Anyway, when Ah Sam get arrested, his wife she can pay that fine to get him outta jail. Then Ah Sam go to Mina with her; run a restaurant there. And way later, he's got another one in Reno, on Main Street. Same as I hear Ah Sam's also in Gardnerville and Bridgeport or Bishop. Yes, sir! So, all over man, Ah Sam." (Mack 139)

Sam Leon's father apparently also lived in the area. According to Corbett:

Sam Leon Bar and Barbershop

"Sam Leon, that's *Pozeeda* Sam's boy…."… "Don't drink. *Pozeeda* Sam. No sir! 'Cause I never did see any them real old-timers doin' that drinkin' or usin' thar *moohoo'oo*… " … " I used to see *Pozeeda* Sam headed from work with a bag of grub the end the day…but he don't say hello to nobody. No sir! Just put his head down and walk past I and my brother like that…." (Mack 215)

Sam Leon knew Jack Wilson, the mystic Paiute prophet known as Wovoka who started a religious movement among many Native Americans, that led to the massacre of many Lakota Sioux at Wounded Knee, South Dakota. In the book, *Wovoka and the Ghost Dance,* Corbett Mack recalls one of the many stories of Wovoka's supernatural powers:

"Sam Leon told me that one time, Jack Wilson worked for Dan Simpson and he digs up a tree. Small tree, you know. Jack Wilson can pack that on his shoulder. But when it starts to rain, Jack, don't even get wet"… "Jacks clothes didn't get wet, either, so I kind of think maybe he makes that rain himself." (Hittman, 338)

In the book, *An Interview with Frank Yparraguirre*, Frank, a Basque hardware store owner for many years, said the following about Sam Leon's Gardnerville establishment:

"He run a gaming casino and a bar and a card place. It would be straight across from where that hardware store is today on Main Street…"

"Well Sam Leon was quite a gambler. He used to like to gamble up there in Bodie before he ever come to Gardnerville. I think that's what enticed a lot of people to go there, because Sam knew how to make money, you know…"

"He must have come here in the early 1920s, I'd say. That's when he came down from Bodie…"

"But Leon made it attractive. He put a little money out, and people always had a tendency to go back in there and play cards, because there was a lot of loose money running around…"

"Send out winners, and you get players." (Yparraguirre 115-116)

In 1928, Sam opened the Kirkwood restaurant in Bridgeport, California. The *Bridgeport Chronicle-Union* noted that he "conducted a restaurant in Gardnerville for several years, and many years ago was chef for one of the hotels in Bodie." He bought the U.S. Hotel of Bodie from George L. Langrill on May 6th, 1930. At this same time his marriage to Gertie was breaking up. He started running notices in the newspaper that he was not responsible for debts contracted by his wife.

The 1930 census shows Sam Leon running the U.S. Hotel with 21 boarders, who were mostly miners. Gertie was living with her sister in Wadesworth, Nevada, and Laura was a pupil at the Carson/Stewart Indian School. Bodie was going through a new resurgence because of the Clinton-West Corporation starting operation. Sam paid Mono County taxes in 1930 for a house in Bodie, and a 1928 Studebaker Coupe. The next year he paid taxes on the U.S. Hotel and a 1930 Ford sedan.

In June of 1930, William O. Walker, prohibition administrator for Nevada, California, and Hawaii paid a visit to Bodie and noted that "Bodie was real lively. Possibly a party of enforcement officers will invade the hills of that district in the near future." On Sunday, September 16th, federal enforcement officers swooped down on

Sam Leon's Bar

Main Street and arrested fourteen people on liquor law violations. Each posted a $1500 bond. The names of those arrested could not be found, but it is interesting that Sam Leon sold property to J. S. Cain shortly after. As luck would have it, the great American humorist, Will Rogers, came into town the next day. He wrote a syndicated column, in some newspapers along with a cartoon of three Bodie saloons, each with two arms coming out of and above their roofs shaking their fists, while the sun was setting amongst the surrounding mountains. His short telegram #1293, which ran in about 500 newspapers as a column titled As Rogers Sees it reported:

> "Mohave Cal., Sept. 16. -Did you ever see a 100 per cent dry town? Well I did, but I had to go to the heart of the desert to do it. It was Bodie, the old mining town that's been lately monkey glanded with a new gold scare. Mrs. Rogers and I blew in there last night. I wanted to show her what a real live western mining town was like at night. Well of all the sad looking messes it was it! The night before, twenty prohibition officers had raided the place and closed her tight. Did you ever see a miner on soda pop? You can't even console him. Every throat was dry and every eye was wet." (Rogers)

On June 23rd, 1932, the great Bodie fire, started by a 2½ year old firebug playing with matches, burnt down all but five businesses in downtown Bodie, including Sam Leon's newly renovated U.S. Hotel. Twenty-four houses were also burnt down, leaving thirty-two people homeless among the 125 people living in Bodie. The June 25th, *Chronicle-Union* reported:

> "Sam Leon, owner of the old U.S. Hotel, took his truck to help move someone's belongings from the fire zone thinking his own property safe and had moved his loaded truck to a safety zone, when his attention was called to the fact that the fire settled down on his hotel building and all he saved, we are informed, was his trunk, the entire building and its contents going up in smoke."

In a swift and incredible change in Sam Leon's luck, the April 29th, 1933, The *Bridgeport Chronicle-Union* ran an article titled "BIG STRIKE MADE AT BODIE";

> "From the famous old mining camp of Bodie, comes the good word of another of those big strikes for which the camp was famous in its better days. Working from the 400 foot level of the old Bodie mine, Bert Davis, Sam Leon and Joe Mosier, struck what is believed to be the old Fortuna vein, famous in its day for its richness."

In *Mining Camp Days*, Emil Billeb tells a story of Sam Leon coming to San Francisco with a Paiute woman and two small children walking behind him single file to collect his share of the old Bodie mine profits from J. S. Cain (Billeb 205). Apparently the strike was short lived. On June 1st, 1937, Sam and his partner Pete Jono of Lee Vining bought what is now called Sam Leon's Bar. On May 8th, 1941, Sam bought the brick hotel building in Bodie from Mary Dechambeau. In 1942, Bodie had a population of three people, of which Sam was one. Afterwards, Sam seemed to hit a string of bad luck. In 1944 Sam got into an automobile accident in Bishop. His room at the Royce rooms in Reno was broken into and a radio and four pints of whiskey were stolen. In 1948 Sam fractured his pelvis in Reno when a car ran into him. In 1953, his car was broken into and a suitcase, two shirts, and some cooks' hats and aprons were stolen in Reno. Finally, Sam died in a Reno hospital on February 20th, 1955, without any known survivors and was buried in Mt. View Cemetery.

Model A Ford by Sam Leon's Bar

Bodie Shoe Shine

Joe Hahner

Joe Hahner was the last barber to work in Bodie. He bought the barber shop from Vic Bernard, the previous barber, in 1911 for $1500. The May 30th, 1911 Nevada State Journal listed it for sale:

"BARBER SHOP SNAP-A two-chair barber shop in Bodie, Cal., is for sale at a bargain. This shop is in the best location possible and has two porcelain bath tubs, with heater, etc. All the equipment is modern and in first-class condition. Only exclusive barber shop in town. Top prices for everything. Bodie has been a good camp for years and with the advent of the Hydro-Electric company's power has taken a new lease of life."

Josef Nicloas Hahner was born in 1881 in Moritzfeld, Hungary, which after World War I became Maureni, Romania. He immigrated to the United States in 1906 when he was twenty-five years old. The manifest of the ship Batavia from Hamburg, Germany, described him as being five foot zero inches tall. He had grey eyes, brown complexion, fair hair, and a pockmarked face. His occupation was listed as a hairdresser. He arrived in New York with forty dollars.

Joe worked in Bodie until late 1927, when he moved to Bridgeport, California. In December of 1927 he started running a regular advertisement for "Joe's Barber Shop" in the *Bridgeport Chronicle-Union*. The ad specified "Ladies and Gents Haircutting," "Childrens Work a Specialty," and "Shaving - Massage." The barber shop was "Open All Year Around." Mono County tax records indicate he drove a 1928 Essex Coupe.

Joe sold the barber shop in Bodie on June 23rd, 1937, to Pete Jono and Sam Leon for ten dollars. He had previously leased the barber shop to Walter R. Laird and then to Mrs. J. R. Hise. Mrs Hise was Hazel Hise's mother. Hazel was a hairdresser.

Joe Hahner never married. He died on October 2nd, 1941 of cardiac failure. His death certificate notes he had suffered from chronic alcoholism for fourteen years. The Reno Evening Gazette on October 14th, 1941, ran his obituary:

"BRIDGEPORT Calif OCT 14-
Joseph Hahner, better known as Joe the Barber, was found dead in his bed in his barber shop by friends Thursday morning. He had been around as usual the evening before and had apparently died in his sleep. He had been a resident of this section for many years, but little is known as his past life. For many years he operated a barber shop in Bodie and about 1928 moved his business here."

Barber Chair

August Soderling

August Soderling was a well known assayer in Bodie. He was born in Sweden in August, 1841. On October, 19th, 1860, he immigrated to the United States. He arrived in New York on the ship Guttenberg, from Hamburg, Germany, with Chicago as his destination. His occupation was listed as a clerk. August worked in Nevada mining camps such as Treasure Hill, and managed the The Theall Co. assay office in Austin, Nevada. By 1878, he was in Bodie, working as an assayer. He never married.

The Soderling assay office was located next to the Sam Leon Bar. It burned down in the 1932 fire. Prior to that, it was located across the street and burned down in the 1892 fire. In 1885, August paid Mono County taxes for a frame house used as an assay office, a musical instrument $30, furniture $25, library $30, and bar steel $30. In later years he paid taxes on various mining claims, assay equipment, machinery, scales, and a bicycle.

A. Soderling held a number patents including U.S. patent 375212 issued on December 20th, 1887, for an *amalgamating-pan*, and U.S. patent 636114, together with J. S. Cain and S. M. MacKnight issued on October 31st, 1899, for *preliminary treatments of ores or tailings before cyaniding*.

Assay Equipment

August Soderling was active in the I.O.O.F. He joined the Wildey Lodge number 1 of Gold Hill, Nevada in 1866, and joined the Bodie Lodge number 279 in 1890, where he served as Vice Grand and trustee. August was a partner in a number of rich strikes, including the California Comstock of the Paterson District near Sweetwater.

The Mono County Index to Insane, lists August Soderling, age 60, as being committed to the Napa State Asylum on October, 15th, 1901. Presumably, he was a victim of mercury poisoning from the various experiments he performed in his research. The *Chronicle-Union* reported:

> "SENT TO NAPA—On Tuesday Judge Virden, on certificates of Dr. Davison of this town, and Dr. Robinson, of Bodie, judged A. Soderling insane and ordered him sent to the Napa Asylum. He was taken to Napa on Thursday by Sheriff Kirkwood and Elmer Kirkwood. Mr. Soderling has been a resident of Bodie for nearly 25 years, and highly respected by all who knew him, and it is to be hoped he will recover from the misfortune that has overtaken him."

Apparently, he recovered because the May 9th, 1903, *Chronicle-Union* reported :

> "A. Soderling, the well known assayer, returned home, Thursday. Mr. Soderling, we are pleased to state, has entirely recovered his health."

After his return, he was given a curious award of the barrel of W. S. Bodey's gun barrel, which was never previously reported as being found. On January 11th, 1908, the *Bridgeport Chronicle-Union* reported that A. Soderling was sick for some time, went to Hawthorne, and that Lester Bell would act in his place.

Clouds - I.O.O.F. Building and Dechambeau Hotel

Henry F. Metzger

Henry Fred Metzger worked as a mill hand for the Standard Mill in Bodie. He was born in November, 1859, in Callicoon, New York. His father, Adam Metzger, was a shoemaker who emigrated from Darmstadt, Germany, in 1854. Henry and his younger brother George came to Bodie in 1878 and worked for the Standard Mill. The stamp mill ran day and night, crushing ore with heavy stamps, which shook the ground and could be heard for miles away.

On October 29th, 1888, he married Lena E. Thompson. Lena and her family emigrated from Denmark and lived near Gardnerville, Nevada. Henry and Lena had five children, all born in Bodie. Their son, Harry M. Metzger, who started painting at the age of 16, called himself "a desert wanderer from Bodie" and was well known for his oil paintings of desert scenes of the West. Henry's younger brother George died in July of 1898 of alcoholism in Bodie.

Standard Mill

In November of 1906, Henry was appointed to foreman of the Standard Mill. After the Standard Consolidated Mining Company dissolved and was sold to J. S. Cain, Henry worked for the Tonopah Extension Mining Company in Tonopah, Nevada. He worked as a battery man in the 30-stamp cyanide mill, adding mercury to the mortar boxes in the amalgamation process. He moved to Reno in 1927. Henry died at his daughter's home on November 15th, 1943, at the age of 84.

The sign in the window of the Metzger House, "La Belle Beauty Shop" is said to have been from a beauty parlor run by Olive Bell. There were people, such as Hazel Hise, who advertised hair permanents with a "combo ringlette" in the *Bridgeport Chronicle-Union and Bodie Chronicle* in the early 1930's. She arranged to use the candy shop in Bodie as a temporary one-day beauty shop. The shop was destroyed in the June 1932 fire.

1925 Nash by the "La Belle Beauty Shop"

Cecil B. Burkham

Cecil Bertrand Burkham is known as the person who brought the automobile to Bodie. He was born on September 22nd, 1878, in Bakersfield, California. His parents, Solomon and Mary, moved to Bodie in 1879, where Solomon worked freighting wood and ore, and later went into the mercantile business. He operated the Burkham Stage Lines with Cecil as a partner and stage coach driver. Solomon was active in Democratic Party politics and ran for state senator. Solomon had a shoot-out with the infamous Carson City gambler, Harry Butts. According to the December 7th, 1895, *Chronicle-Union*:

> ANOTHER—Another shooting racket is being examined into at Bodie, S. B. Burkham of Bodie, and Harry Butts of Carson, being the principals, the trouble growing out of the late races in Bodie. As there are all sorts of stories about the affair, we must await the result of the examination. It is enough to say that no one was killed, or even hit.

A jury trial, Burkham vs. Butts, was held the next May, and Harry Butts was released.

The stage coach, mail route, and mercantile businesses were lucrative. In 1892, the rate from Bridgeport to Bodie was $2.50 and a penny a pound for freight. Solomon died at the age of 49 in January of 1904, and was buried in Bodie. His wife Mary moved to San Francisco, and later Reno. She died on January 7th, 1945 at the age of 84. She wanted to be buried in Bodie, which she considered her home. Cecil arranged for her burial on Memorial Day, 1945 in Bodie, where about fifty people attended. Cecil ran the Burkham Mercantile Company and converted the horse drawn into an automobile stage business. In 1904, he married Josephine Seiler, had two boys, Frank and Cecil, and in 1910 was living in the Burkham House on Mill Street. In 1914, Cecil moved to Hawthorne and was awarded the mail route from Hawthorne to Bridgeport via Bodie. He owned the Burkham Garage, a Dodge automobile dealership, and delivered a number of new automobiles to people in Bodie. In 1914, the *Reno Evening Gazette* ran an article titled "Parcels Piling Up":

> Walker Lake Bulletin : Cecil Burkham, mail contractor from Hawthorne to Bodie, informed the Bulletin that he has carried an average of 1,750 pounds of parcel post daily from Hawthorne post office. There are now about five tons of accumulated parcel post packages there awaiting removal. In addition to the regular automobiles, Mr. Burkham has a four horse wagon constantly on the road, and yet he cannot move the stuff, as fast as it arrives.

Cecil had a sharp tongue, as the January 15th, 1919, *Reno Evening Gazette* article titled "SUES RANCHER FOR ALLEGED REMARKS" indicates:

> "Women held their ears and left the lobby, when they heard the remarks Cecil Burkham made about Sam Nelson according to the complaint filed in district court by Nelson, in which he asks for a judgment of $25,000 against Burkham for damages to his reputation and business.

In 1919, Cecil no longer had the stage business, and went into ranching. He owned several large cattle ranches and later the Consolidated Warehouse and the Reno Feed and Seed Co. He moved to Reno in 1921. Cecil retired in 1952, and died at the age of 93 in a Reno hospital on December 31st, 1971.

Burkham House on Mill Street

August Seiler

August Seiler lived in what is now called the Seiler House on Park Street in Bodie, and was the proprietor of the Seiler Saloon on the corner of Main and Union streets. The saloon burnt down during the 1932 fire which started behind the Sawdust Saloon across the street. According to miscellaneous notes provided by the Seiler family, August was born in Basel, Switzerland on February 20th, 1845, and had five brothers and sisters. The youngest, Francesca became a nun in Milwaukee. In 1872, when he was 27 years old, he came to San Francisco. Three years later, he married Theresa Dresel from Buhlertal, Germany on October 14th, 1875. They had two children, August and George, who died as young children.

August was an owner of the National Hotel in San Francisco, which he sold in 1879, to try his luck prospecting in Bodie. Theresa stayed behind to give birth to their daughter Hermene on January 26th, 1880, the day after their son George died, and joined August in Bodie in the spring. They lived in a house across the street from the Methodist Church, and moved into the "Seiler House" three years later. Although they wanted to buy the house, the owner did not want to sell it. They kept the house as a residence until 1914, when Theresa died.

In 1882, August became a naturalized citizen. The Seilers had three more children: Josephine born on October 2nd, 1881, in Bodie, Pauline on September 10th, 1883 in Bridgeport, and Gustav, on January 10th, 1888, in Bodie. Tragically, Gustav, nicknamed Gussie, died on December 22nd, 1891, and is buried in Bodie. Pauline Seiler McKeough is also buried in Bodie. Josephine married Cecil Burkham on May 18th, 1904, and lived in the Burkham House on Mill Street. Seiler's saloons were popular. A *Chronicle-Union* article reported:

"Johnnie Andrews was out in the hills the other day and captured a Mono Lake champagne-acorn fed porker and is now loading it up on mushrooms and tobacco sauce and will serve it at the Seiler saloon next Wednesday evening. It will be trimmed in the latest gastronomic fashion and served free to patrons and guests. Don't miss it."

Child's Grave - Bodie Cemetery

August had a number successful of mining claims. Some of them were named after his daughters. The claims were near Masonic, another ghost town in Mono County. The November 1904, *Chronicle-Union* articles reported:

"It was reported on the street last night that August Seiler of Bodie has struck ore in the Hermene at Masonic that worked $2.50 a pound and had two men working it in a mortar.
August Seiler has four men at work building a house and preparing for winter. The tunnel now in about 50 feet will be rapidly forced ahead. This claim has one of the best showings in the district."

Other claims he had were the Red Top (formerly the Pauline), the New Era, the East Josephine

Consolidated Group of Mines, commonly known and called the "Tunnel Group," and comprising the East Josephine, The Baltic, and the Carparthia. Besides several cabins, he also had a combination store and hotel built on Main Street of Lower Town Masonic. Apparently, he spent his time back and forth in both Bodie and Masonic. A *Chronicle-Union* article reported in November, 1909:

> "August Seiler has finished his assessment work and returned to Bodie last Thursday. Harvey Boone moved him back."

Theresa died in San Francisco on April 13th, 1914 at her daughter's home. After her death, August lived in Masonic until his health also declined.

On Friday, September 3rd, 1915, a special election was called by the Board of Supervisors of Mono County for an ordinance where alcohol could not be sold in saloons. Ironically, the board extended liquor licences to saloon owners at the same time they were deciding to hold the vote. The ordinance won by a vote of 183 to 125; thus Bodie became officially "dry" four years before it became "bone dry" when the Volstead Act was passed to enforce the Eighteenth Amendment. Bodie was the only precinct that voted against the ordinance by the surprisingly slim margin of 49 to 44.

The February 26th, 1916 *Bridgeport Chronicle-Union* reported on a "Raid at Masonic":

Seiler House Porch

> "Last week Sheriff Dolan made a raid at Masonic and as a result Florence Olague was arrested charged with keeping a gambling house and a public place where alcoholic liquors are sold; and August Seiler arrested on two complaints charged with keeping a public place where alcoholic liquors are sold. Olague plead guilty to both charges last Saturday and was fined $200 and placed on six months probation. On Monday morning Seiler was sentenced to pay a fine of $200 and placed on six months probation."

August died on June 5th, 1919, in San Francisco. Both Theresa and August are buried in the Holy Cross Cemetery in Colma, California.

Horace F. Swasey

Horace Swasey was a rancher near Yerington, Nevada, who bought the two story frame building containing six rooms that is now know as the Swazey Hotel. The outside of the quintessential building of the Old West used to have stairs that went up to the second floor on the side it leans to until about the 1940's. The building was bought by Horace F. Swasey for ninety dollars in gold coin on November 9th, 1894 from Nelson Poli of Esmeralda County, Nevada. The spelling of the name "Swasey" was used interchangeably with "Swazey" and "Swayze", with "Swasey" used most often. Nelson had bought the building, which was erected some time after the 1892 fire from James Perry of Bodie the previous year.

Horace Fairbanks Swasey was born in Vermont on May, 30th, 1835. His parents, Henneneal and Eliza Swasey, moved shortly after to the Iowa Territory.

Horace had a hot temper and a colorful past. According to the 1863 *Washoe Times* newspaper, Horace shot and killed George Derickson, the editor of the *Washoe Times*. The shooting occurred on January 23rd, 1863. The next day, the *Washoe Times* reported:

Back of the Swazey Hotel

> "Tragical.
> Yesterday morning, about half past nine o'clock, George W. Derickson, the proprietor of this newspaper was MURDERED!
> The examination of the murderer at the moment we are writing this is in progress before the proper court, and our veneration for the majesty of the law prevents us from speaking as we feel."
> "The examination of H. F. Swayze, the prisoner was commenced yesterday afternoon before Justice Chillseo."

There are several versions of how the shooting came about. The reason for the shooting is probably best described the July 13th, 1895 edition of the *Weekly Nevada State Journal*, in a Washoe City reminiscence article:

"During the Winter of 1862, one G, W. Derickson established the *Washoe Times*, a weekly publication. He was killed soon after by a man by the name of Horace F. Swazey, who lived at Ophir, and the paper then went into the hands of General Allen, uncle of Mr. Derickson. The killing was the result of a wordy altercation in the printing office, near the middle of the day, where Swazey went to demand a retraction by the editor for abusive language published concerning him. Swazey as a correspondent at Ophir had plagiarized by copying a funny article from an Eastern paper and tried to palm it on the *Times*, as original. In this he signally failed and Mr. Derickson exposed the writer in the next issue of the paper and charged him with being an imbecile and an ass. This caused Swazey to demand a retraction. Both men were armed but the Editor being a man of more than ordinary nerve, drove Swazey out of the office. Swazey retreated up the street and several hours afterward, seeing Derickson outside of his office on the sidewalk, he deliberately fired from in front of the McFarland Livery Stable, a distance of more than a hundred yards, and killed the Editor on the spot. Swazey got out of town and escaped to Sierra Valley, but some weeks later was arrested and indicted. On his trial he was ably defended by Charley De Long and finally went free. He is still residing in Nevada."

The fact is that he was found guilty of manslaughter and served time in the Nevada State Prison in 1863. Another version of how the shooting actually transpired was reprinted in the January 31st, 1863, *Washoe Times* which quoted the *Virginia Union*:

Front of the Swazey Hotel

"Derickson ordered him out of the house. He started backwards towards the door, reaching behind as if to draw a pistol; whereupon Derickson drew his derringer and fired, the ball striking Swayze's chin, breaking his jaw and carrying away two of his teeth, which, with the ball, he afterward spat out. He then turned and ran out, pursued by Derickson, who drew a five-shooter and fired an ineffectual shot. Upon this Swayze turned and fired; the first ball struck a bystander in the leg; the second went through the heart of Derickson, killing him instantly."

The *Washoe Times* claimed the above account was incorrect, and that Swazey drew his gun first and both fired simultaneously. The *Times* also noted that Horace used "Swazey" in correspondence with the newspaper and that his neighbors in Sherwin's Gulch said he used the spelling "Swasey" uniformly in all written transactions.

After being released from prison in 1866, Horace F. Swazey was married to Margaret E. Callehan on September 14th, 1868, in Esmeralda County, Nevada. Together they had four sons and three daughters. Swasey worked his ranch in Mason Valley, typically harvesting four hundred tons of hay. After he bought the Swazey Hotel, he moved to Bodie. He paid Mono County taxes on the hotel, a stable next door to it, and a cabin, as well as about $300 worth of general merchandise that he apparently sold out of the building. The *Nevada State Journal* referred to Horace F. Swasey as a leading Bodie merchant.

The August 29th, 1892 edition of the *Reno Evening Gazette* reported on Horace's daughter, Elenora:

"Frank Hansbrongh Deserts His Young Wife in a Most Cruel and Cowardly Manner."

"Mrs. Frank Hansbrousih, formerly Miss Nellie Swasey, is the daughter of a thrifty rancher in Mason Valley. About two years ago she met the person to whom she was married some time in June in Virginia City, and who was traveling agent for a nursery firm in the East. On the 20th of this month, Harisbrough left his young wife at the Golden Eagle Hotel in this city, telling her that he was going east and would return in a short time. He wrote to her parents from Ogden, telling them to go and get their daughter, as he had left her and was going to South Africa. There had been no trouble between the newly married pair, and when the husband left he evinced none but the most affectionate feeling towards his wife, and the news of his desertion came upon her like a clap of thunder from a cloudless sky, as she maintains that not even so much as a cross word had ever passed between them. His people live in Louisville, Ky., and he travelled for a nursery firm in Bloomington, Ill.

It was a most cruel and cowardly desertion, and it will be strange if the vengeance of Heaven, if not of man, does not overtake the stony-hearted wretch for his infamous act. Mr. and Mrs. Swasey came to Reno Saturday, and yesterday left with their daughter for their home in Mason Valley. It is the opinion of the parents that Hansnrongh expected to get a considerable amount of money from them, and being disappointed, left her, probably to search for some other victim."

On June 6th, 1900, Nelson Poli, who sold the hotel to Horace Swasey, married his eighteen year old daughter, Gertrude Swasey. Nelson was a forty-year old rancher who emigrated from Italy in 1878. Horace's youngest son, George B. Swasey, and Miss Florence Belle Strosnider of Mason Valley were married in Bodie in November, 1901. They lived in Tonopah, Nevada, where they ran a rooming house. George was the chief of the Tonopah Fire Department. They divorced in 1912. In the 1920's, Florence became involved with Republican Party politics, and became a member of the Nevada State Assembly in 1924 for one term.

In an article titled "Former Resident of Bodie Passes Away", the July 21st, 1906 *Bridgeport Chronicle Union* reported:

"News was received here this week that H. F. Swasey, formerly of this valley, died on the 25th of last month at Manayunk, Pa., after an illness of some two months. Mr. Swasey left this valley, where he had resided many years some two years ago. He was residing at the time of his death at the home of his eldest son, Horace."

Swazey Hotel

DR. JOHN A. STREET

Doctor John Archibald Street was the company physician for the Treadwell Yukon Mining Company, Ltd. in Bodie between December of 1930 and January of 1932. He was born in Missouri about 1885. His parents were Canadian of Scotch decent. Between 1891 and 1927, he lived in Toronto, Canada, and received his medical degree at McGill University in Montréal in June of 1919. By 1930, Dr. Street was renting a house in Hawthorne, Nevada. He was a 45 years, married to 38 year old Sophia M. Street, who was born in Canada, as were her parents. They had been married 3 years. The following are items from the *Bridgeport Chronicle-Union and Bodie Chronicle* during the Bodie years:

"Dr. Street, formerly of Hawthorne, now of Alameda, has accepted the work of physician for the Treadwell Yukon Company and is expected to arrive at Bodie to take up his duties sometime this week."

"The Treadwell Yukon Company is building an addition to the office of its physician, Dr. Street, which is to be used as a recovery room for men injured at the mines."

"Dr. Street, our local physician, is sporting a new Studebaker Six automobile."

"Dr. Street, one day this week, about made up his mind that he was short one perfectly fine police dog. The Doctor hunted all over town and when he could not find the animal, went down to Hawthorne to take a look-see in that town, but still was unable to find his dog. Dr. Street came home having about made up his mind that his pal was gone for keeps. He went to bed and sometime during the night, his dog returned, weary and footsore to his master. Probably, the dog was stolen and taken quite a distance in a car and made his get-away for home the first opportunity he had."

1932 was not a good year for Bodie. The Treadwell Yukon abandoned Bodie after only a few years of operation. There was an extremely bitter winter with drifts of snow up to 20 feet. People were snowbound with a shortage of food. There was no bread, butter, milk or eggs left. The only way out of Bodie was on skies or snowshoes. On January 3rd, a fire broke out in an old laundry building, threatening the whole downtown, and foreshadowing the great fire that would occur later that summer. Frozen pipes prevented extinguishing the fire. Three buildings were burnt down and two people, Mr. and Mrs. Roy Griffith, were treated by the doctor for frozen feet as they had to jump out of the buildings in their night clothes. The town had already been isolated for 12 days. On January 5th, mountaineers came in to rescue a dozen people from Bodie. By the end of January, Dr. Street called it quits. From the January 29th, *Reno Evening Gazette*:

" Dr. John A. Street of Bodie, has closed his office in that camp and will spend a few days here, then proceed to Los Angeles where he expects to engage in practice. Dr. Street was able to get out of Bodie by way of Bridgeport and Sweetwater and states that the road down Del Monte Canyon will not be opened for some time to come."

Instead of moving to Los Angeles, Dr. Street emigrated from the United States to Canada in March of 1932. His destination was his mother's home in Toronto,

Dr. Street Examination Table

EMMA GOLDSMITH

Emma Goldmith was a prostitute and madam in Bodie. Her establishment was known as the Osark. When she died, the October 13th, 1900, edition of the Bridgeport *Chronicle-Union* printed a short and cruelly harsh epitaph:

"DEAD.—Emma Goldsmith, one of Bodie's lowest levels, died about 3 o'clock this morning."

Dr. J. E. Cox recorded her death on the next day, and noted she was a Bodie housewife, forty-two years old, a native of California, and that she died of congestion of the lungs. It is not clear where Emma came from. Emma's descendants list a variety places, including that she was born in Baltimore, Maryland in 1858. None, it appears has any strongly held conviction or data.

In the book Rosa May: *The Search For A Mining Camp Legend*, George Williams III included a letter from Emma Goldsmith written to Rosa May on August 15th, 1879. Emma wrote that she was almost sobered when she received a letter with a San Jose postmark. This suggests that she may have had family or acquaintances living there. His book, *The Red Light Ladies of Virginia City*, has a photo of the "pencil written letter by Emma, perhaps Emma Goldsmith". Williams believed that Emma used the name Emma Hall, who was listed twice in the 1880 census in Virginia City; once on June 16th living next door to Cad Thompson, a Virginia City madam that Rosa May worked for, and a week later in jail. Another name descendants say Emma may have used is Emma Comstock.

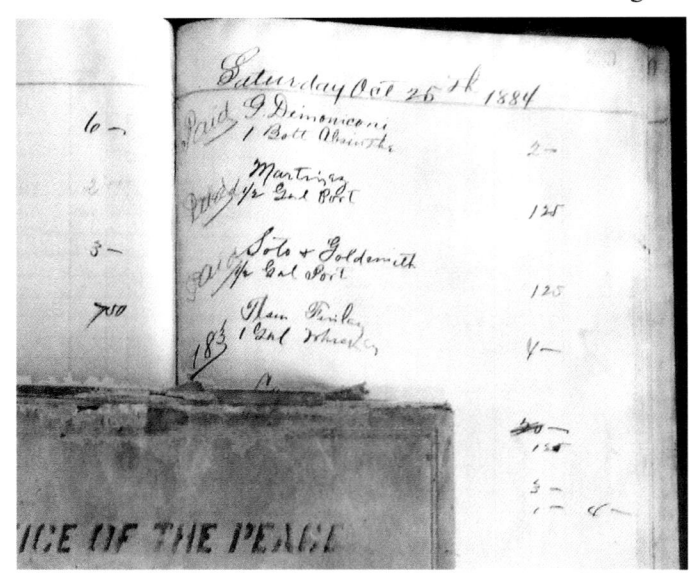

Bodie Museum Liquor Log - Soto & Goldsmith

The 1870 census shows a twenty-two year old Emma Goldsmith living in San Jose with a family whose head was William Goldsmith, an engraver. She would have been fifty-two when she died. By 1880, the Goldsmiths moved to San Francisco. William Goldsmith was arrested in September, 1896 for passing bogus bills. The 1860 census for the Goldsmiths in San Francisco lists Emma as Emma Coons, suggesting she may have been adopted. Another reference of Emma Goldsmith living in Northern California is a December 22nd, 1880, article in the *San Francisco Chronicle* titled "EXPENSIVE EMMA, And the Jewels Which She Considered Necessaries.":

"Justice Connelly's Court was yesterday the center of attraction for a crowded audience, which convened for the purpose of listening to evidence in the case of Rudolf Kosche vs. Joseph Goetz, which involved the liability of defendant to pay for goods supplied to a certain Emma Goldsmith, who deemed her relations with defendant to have been of a sufficiently marital character to render his payment of her necessary debts legally just. It appeared from the evidence produced by plaintiff, that prior to a trip to Europe, from which he has only shortly returned, Mr. Goetz has been rusticating with the fair Emma at a place of resort near Sonoma City known as Nathanson's Park, and at this rural retreat had permitted her to mix in the society of the place as Mrs. Goetz, and that under this name she had purchased goods amounting to $143 from one Enricht, who had assigned his claim to Kosche, the plaintiff in the present action. The defense, on the other hand, argued that though Goetz considered himself fairly liable for the four square meals per diem which it transpired Emma disposed of at the Sonoma ranch, he objected to paying the bills she contracted during his absence including as they did, 1 gold ring $3.50; cash $20; cash, $15; 1 diamond ear ring $27.50; 2 lace collars $22; 1 turquoise ring $16.50; 3 pieces duchesse lace $21.50, and various other items which seemed to partake rather of the character of luxuries than necessities. Plaintiff's council sought to show that the baronial presence and reported substance of defendant were perfectly sufficient to entitle Emma to such expenditures, and the use of diamonds in certain stations of life was as imperative as that of bread and butter to others..."

In 1882, Jospeh Goetz was arrested in San Francisco for smuggling 500 pounds of opium. He died in 1907 at the age of 78 leaving an estate of half a million dollars in cash and real estate in Chinatown.

In Bodie, tax records indicate Emma owned a house in Bodie on lot 70, block 21, from 1893 through 1900, along with twenty-five dollars in furniture, and an organ. In August, 1895, the *Hawthorne Bulletin* wrote:

> "Miss Emma Goldsmith, a female of undoubted character, took three shots at Harry Butts, a sporting man on Monday. None of the shots took effect."

Harry Butts was someone who was always in trouble. He was a gambler who owned race horses and was involved in a number of shootings and thefts. He went to prison for two years for passing counterfeit money and was involved with opium since he was a juvenile in Carson City.

Ella Cain wrote about Emma Goldsmith, who "boarded out her little boy to a family named Stewart." Emma's descendents say his name was Murray Irving Scott. Family legend is that Emma claimed that the father was a son of Irving Scott, the industrialist who was the head of the Union Iron Works, which built most of the machinery used in the Comstock, and won Navy contracts to build ships at the Potrero Shipyard in San Francisco. He built battleships of the Great White Fleet such as the Oregon, California, and Ohio.

Murry Irving Scott was born in Oakland on July 29th, in "1887 or 1889". Emma sent her son to live with a family in Grass Valley, California when he was five years old. The 1900 census shows him as ten year old Stewart Steward living with the Watson family. When he was 17 or 18 he got in a fight and hit his opponent, who then fell down, hit his head, and died. He fled to Mexico, and changed his name to Fred Fulton when he returned. Fred married Ora Frances Lemmon in 1943. They had many children before he deserted his family. He died in 1978 after living in Grass Valley, California. One of Fred's great granddaughters, April Hawley, remembers him when she was a little girl with this touching vignette:

> "I remember he was small and quiet except when he played his harmonica which he did quite often to make me happy. I remember it was a very large harmonica not like the ones that you commonly see now; anyways he played it very masterfully and could play anything. My mother and I would drive out to Grass Valley and pick him up from a Hotel that he lived at I remember walking along the old wooden boardwalks to get him and we would bring him back to our house in Shingle Springs to stay with us for the weekend."

ROSA MAY

Rosa May was the queen of the red light district of Bodie. According to the 1900 U.S. Census, Rosa was born in Pennsylvania in January, 1855, of Irish parents. She was single, living in Bodie in the red light district, and listed her occupation as a seamstress. The 1910 census listed her as Rosie May, born in 1864 in Pennsylvania of Irish parents, and listed her occupation as a prostitute. She had only aged one year from 45 to 46 in ten years! Mono County property records show she bought the house, that she lived in for "upwards of ten years", on June 14th, 1902 for $175, indicating she may have lived in Bodie on the west side of Bonanza Street from around 1882 or earlier. Mono County taxes were last paid for her house and fifty dollars worth of furniture on November 25th of 1911. Tax records show her house was sold to the state on June 23rd, 1913. A week prior, the *Bridgeport Chronicle-Union* listed her property:

> "No. 202. Rosa May: Bodie school district: Lot in Bodie, lot 40, block 26, value $10, improvements house value $200: total value $210: total tax $4.72, Bodie fire tax $1.05; first installment $2.36, 1.5 per cent penalty 35 cents, second installment $2.36, 5 percent delinquency 24 cents, costs $1.00: Total amount due and delinquent..... $7.36"

In his facinating book, *Rosa May: The Search For A Mining Camp Legend*, George Williams III tells of his research of Rosa May. He located several dozen letters that Ella Cain's daughter possessed which were written to Rosa in Carson and Virginia cities by various people and included them in his book. Most were written by her lover, Ernest Marks, a saloon keeper. The dates of the letters were between September 27th, 1876 and March 27th, 1880. Williams followed Rosa's life during this time in the Nevada brothels of Carson and Virginia Cities and concluded that Rosa's real name was Rosa Elizabeth White, born in 1855 in Pennsylvania of Irish parents. There was no explanation in his book of how he concluded her name was Rosa Elizabeth White, although Rosa May's birthplace and birth date were based on the 1900 census. The 1880 U.S. Census does show a Rosa E. White, 27 years old, living in Carson City with Jennie Moore, 54, and Mary A. Phillips, 58. Both were mentioned in the Williams book as madams for whom Rosa May worked. Rosa E. White was listed as a dressmaker born in 1853 in Maine with both parents born in New Hampshire. Mrs. Phillips was mentioned in a letter to Rosa May from Emma Goldsmith, Rosa's friend and another prostitute that moved to Bodie. One of the letters was addressed to Rosa May in Carson City, in care of Jennie Moore, a black woman born in Ireland.

To make matters even more confusing, Ella Cain's book, *The Story of Bodie*, has Rosa May born in France, and there are newspaper accounts of Rosa Olague, "The Castilian Cypriot," who slashed Bill Green in the face with a knife. She is sometimes confused with Rosa May and referred to as Rosa May Olague.

Delinquent property tax records led Williams to conclude that Rosa died between November of 1911 and 1912. Based on a 1927 Burton Frasher photograph that includes a grave outside the cemetery fence, and the tale of Rosa May in Ella Cain's *The Story of Bodie*, Williams built a wooden fence around where he thought Rosa May was buried. The new grave fence was about 150 feet from a cement maker that Louis Serventi erected around 1965, which Serventi made to fulfill a promise made to his uncle Antonio, who used to live next to Rosa May. The photograph titled "The Two Graves of Rosa May" shows the cement marker and the wooden fence.

The Two Graves of Rosa May

Ella Cain wrote that Rosa May died while nursing sick miners during a pneumonia epidemic. While there was no known pneumonia epidemic at the time of Rosa's death, an article in the July 29th, 1892, edition of the *San Francisco Chronicle* titled "Bodie of the Past" said that a "terrible epidemic of pneumonia set in and carried away large numbers of the men who were known as the 'all nighters', men who did no work, but prayed on their fellows. One day there were eight funerals in a population of 1200. The people were aghast at the visitation."

Ernest Marks, Rosa's lover, lived in Gold Hill, several miles from Virginia City when he wrote the letters to Rosa. He was born in Germany around 1850. In 1900, Ernest was a saloon keeper in Bodie. He suffered from rheumatism for much of his life. The 1907 *Chronicle-Union* reported "Ernest Marks is still fighting the rheumatism. Dr. Franklin is in attendance with his galvanic battery and if this does not afford relief he will have a wire brought from the Standard electric plant." Ernest died in July of 1928 and was buried in the Odd Fellows Cemetery by Billy Owens, the last undertaker of Bodie. After his death, Billy possessed Rosa's trunk of letters and clothing until his death in 1933, when Ella Cain bought it, and displayed some of the contents in the Bodie Museum. Ella wrote that Marks pulled a gun on Billy when he proposed a toast to Rosa May, and that later they would become friends, with Billy taking care of Marks.

Bodie Morgue

In the November 1929, issue of *Touring Topics*, Carl Parcher Russell, the chief naturalist of Yosemite National Park who earned a Ph.D. in Ecology, wrote an article titled "The Bodie That Was" which described the history and folklore of Bodie. He had interviewed Jim Cain for most of the story. He had also interviewed and wrote about Ernest Marks for whom he used the pseudonym "Smith" in the story and "Rosemary" for Rosa May. Ernest was not very forthcoming, but did show him a polished gold and quartz match case with a naturally formed letter "R". The story told of how "Smith' took on a number of mistresses after "Rosemary's" death, each of which absconded with jewelry that Rosa May left him.

By 1930, only two years after Ernest Mark's death, Rosa May was already a legend. Her grave had already completely vanished after only three years since Burton Frasher photographed it. On August 31st, 1930, a *Los Angeles Times* article by Harry Carr appeared, complete with drawings of Rosa May, and using the name "Al Marks" as a pseudonym for Ernest Marks, and someone named "Al Beaumont", who guided him through the town. This was probably a pseudonym for a odd man named Al Belmont, who was arrested a number of times for brawling. When local prohibition took effect in Bodie, Al filed a complaint against Ernest Marks for serving liquor. A similar article appeared in the November 16th, 1930, edition of the *Oakland Tribune* titled "Ghost Towns Answer World's Cry For Gold":

"It is just as though the scene were shifted back into the '50s. Money is jingling on the gambling tables. Houris again stir memories of Rosie May, once queen of the Bodie red-light district. The old jail, which once more or less confined the "Bad Man of Bodie" famous in song and story, has been occupied again. But-it is now a tame lodging-house for miners."

"Al Beaumont contends he never was one of the bad men, although he carried a brace of guns. He didn't want to feel naked in Bodie. He admits having been in jail twice. Once was for riding his horse into Al Marks's Saloon and breaking the swinging doors when he came out; once for hitching his horse to a lady's piano. He says he had a swell time in jail. His friends kept him supplied by emptying their bottles into his tin cup through the bars."

"Search for the grave of Rosie May has proved futile. Al says she had the grandest funeral in the history of Bodie, but she couldn't be buried in consecrated ground, nor in the Odd Fellows cemetery, and the boys didn't think it would be right to plant Rosie May in the Chinese cemetery. So they buried her in a grave outside the fence. The grave has been lost-obliterated by the desert rains and swept by the mountain winds."

"Rosie May had a lot of diamonds which she bequeathed to her husband, Al Marks. Time healed his wounds and he married another girl, who eloped with many of Rosie's diamonds. With shining faith he married another one and she got away with more diamonds. So Al Marks kept marrying beauteous young ladies who kept eloping with Rosie's diamonds. He died a year or so ago in the little room next to his old saloon with Rosie May's picture looking down upon him. This picture hung there during the entire ghost-town era unnoticed by the throng of souvenir hunters. Steve, the bartender next door, recently took it and placed it over his bar."

Bodie Jail

In a similar article, it was said that when Rosa May was "in her cups", she would sweep into Marks' saloon, Marks would disappear, and she would confront the crowd singing in a voice like the Valkyries:

> "I'm from Texas and I'm one of the boys.
> I'm from Texas and I don't fear no noise."

Ernest Marks, in fact never did marry. Ella Cain wrote that Ernest's last request, that he be buried next to Rosa May, was granted, and that Billy Owens himself dug his grave. Official Mono County records indicate that Ernest was buried inside the cemetery fence. His marker as well (as many others) cannot be found. It may be that Billie Owens dug up Rosa, and buried her with Ernest, or buried Ernest with Rosa outside the fence. Some believe that Rosa was never buried in Bodie. According to George Williams III, Clarence Birks, who was the Cain's watchman, thought Rosa died in Carson City, and was later reburied in Bodie. There do not appear to be death records for Rosa May or Rosa White at the approprate age in either Mono County or Carson City records.

Patrick Reddy

Pat Reddy is known as the famous one armed defense lawyer of Bodie. He was born on February 15th, 1839, in Woonsocket, Rhode Island of Irish parents, Michael and Catherine Reddy, who immigrated to the United States two years prior along with three daughters. They had eight children. Pat came to California at the age of 22 with his 18 year old brother Edward, and worked in mines in Contra Costa County, Placerville, and in Nevada. Edward, a gambler who played the guitar and killed six men in shootouts, opened a gambling house in Cerro Gordo. Pat was equally wild until 1863, when he was shot while walking down a street in Virginia City. An August 11th, 1883, *Weekly Nevada State Journal* article about the shooting titled "A Relic of Early Days" commented on a *Carson Daily Independent* article twenty years prior:

"an account is given of a cowardly attempt by a gang of roughs to assassinate Pat Reddy, the noted lawyer, from which Reddy escaped by a miracle with his life but had his right arm so badly shattered with bullets that it had to be amputated. None but old timers can fully appreciate early life in Nevada."

Reddy House and Quill - Bodie Reenactment

After he lost his arm, he married Emily M. Page in Esmeralda County, Territory of Nevada, on February 8th, 1864. They never had children, although Emily had a daughter, Sybil Josephine Page. Pat studied law in California and was admitted to the bar in 1867. He was known as having an incredible ability in convincing a jury to finding his clients not guilty of murder in shootout cases.

In 1878, Pat was elected as a delegate to the California Constitutional Convention, representing Inyo and Mono counties. He came to Bodie in 1879 and lived there until 1881 when he moved to San Francisco. He was a generous man. He would defend people without money, and would help miners who were down on their luck.

He was appointed a member of the Board of State Prison Directors. In 1883, he was elected to the state senate and served for four years as the representative of Mono, Inyo, Kern, Tulare, and Fresno counties. He became part owner in a number of paying mines and was one of the original owners of the rich Yellow Aster Mine.

Pat died on June 26th, 1900 in his home in San Francisco after suffering from Bright's disease. Emily died in 1904. Her brother was Judge Norman H. Conklin of San Diego. Her daughter, Sybil J. Coleman was the administrix of her estate.

Morning

THEODORE J. HOOVER

Theodore Jesse Hoover, the older brother of the President, was the manager of the Standard Consolidated Mine in Bodie. He was born in West Branch, Iowa, on January 28th, 1871. In 1899, he married Mildred Crew Brooke, while they both attended Stanford University. In 1901, he graduated with a degree in Geology and Mining. They moved to Bodie with their daughter Mildred in 1903 and lived in the company house next to the stamping mill in what is now known as the Hoover House. Theodore worked as an assistant manager, and was promoted a year later. In time, the family got to like the roar from the nearby mill.

Mildred recorded her impressions of Bodie in an unpublished 1940 manuscript titled *Reminiscences of Mildred Crew Brooke Hoover*. She apparently was a patron of Eli Johl of the City Market, who had shot his mining partner:

Hoover House

"The train took us over the Sierra to Reno and then down to the little station of Hawthorne where we completed our journey of 40 miles of stage to Bodie, once the maddest, wildest, and biggest mining camp in California. The old saying "the bad man from Bodie" has originated here and some of the bad men were still there. Our butcher was one of these of whom they said "he had killed his man." I found the butcher a good tradesman after he learned that any poor meat he sent to me was returned to him at once. Many times he sent us sweetbreads free of charge, for no other family cared for them. I have not found that service elsewhere." (Hoover, M 52)

She befriended a dainty young Paiute girl named Minnie and her grandmother, who sold her a water jug made of roots. The grandmother did the family washing, her daughter did ironing, and Minnie came to live with the Hoovers and attend school. She learned to do household chores and was a companion to their young daughter. Mrs. Hoover was interested in learning the Paiute language and would record the words phonetically that Minnie would translate for her. She communicated her findings with professors back at Stanford. The activity gave her the mental outlet she needed.

In 1904, the Hoovers ran an ad in the Chronicle-Union: "WANTED--A good, fresh milk cow. Address T. J. Hoover, Bodie." Apparently they got their cow. In Theodore's unpublished *Memoranda Being a Statement by an Engineer*, he describes his experiences while in Bodie, including a number of camping adventures. The Hoovers went camping each summer in a first class camp they established in Green Creek Canyon, about 9 miles above the hydroelectric station. They invited a number of people to join them, including people from the University. In 1905, the second summer of their stay, they took their cow to camp. Theodore writes about the cow, "She always lived on the desert, and never before had two blades of grass in her mouth at once. Now she was up to her knees in tender grass, and as a result she was dead next morning." (Hoover, T 129)

Two lakes in the region that Theodore explored and mapped were named the Hoover Lakes in his honor, and the region was named the Hoover Wilderness in honor of President Herbert Hoover.

In 1905, after Herbert Hoover returned from China, "Bert" and his wife Lou, "Tad" and Mildred went on a camping trip with pack animals from Bodie to the peak of Tioga Pass. During the trip, one of the party's pack horses fell off a canyon. After rolling nine times down the 200 foot canyon into a willow thicket, scattering "ladies' lingerie, tinned meat, biscuits, knives, forks, plates, and toilet articles", the horse amazingly only had a few cuts. On the way back, Lou and Mildred identified 125 different varieties wildflowers near Bodie.

Theodore improved the Standard, making it one of the most modern of the time, including crushing in cyanide solution, further crushing in "tube mill", and final treatment by the Moore process. The book Bodie *The Mines Are Looking Well...*" describes these processes (Piatt 218-222).

In January of 1906, Bodie had the deepest snow in many years. Theodore was snow blinded during coyote shooting and could not see for several weeks. While still blinded, he received a telegram from the London firm of Bewick, Moreing & Co., offering him a position, which he accepted, of examining engineer for mining activities in Mexico. The Hoovers left Bodie after a blizzard with the snow as high as the tops of the telephone poles in several sleds along with Cecil Berkham and mail that was a week late. The Mildreds were in a large sled with high sides heated by hot rocks and water bottles packed in straw and covered with canvas. After 10 miles in 10 hours, they made it below the snow line. Theodore noted that the country was just as described in Mark Twain's book *Roughing It* (Hoover, T 131).

While Theodore was in Mexico, the Mildreds were in Palo Alto where they experienced the great earthquake of 1906.

Theodore, Mildred and two daughters moved to London where his brother was living. Theodore worked as the general manager of Minerals Separation, Ltd., which was developing the froth flotation process. In 1919 he became a professor at Stanford, and in 1925 he became Dean of the School of Engineering, until he retired in 1936.

Mildred died in 1940, and Theodore died in 1955. They are buried on private property within Rancho Del Oso-Waddell Valley, an area in Santa Cruz County, California, where the Hoovers bought property in 1914.

Standard Mill Office

Rosie McDonald Moose

Rosie McDonald Moose was born in Bodie and lived in what is now called the Indian House. She was born on July 2nd, 1897, and died on July 29th, 1984, in a care center in Big Pine, California. The 1910 census listed her as thirteen year old Rosie McDonald, living in Bodie with her mother, Katie McDonald, a thirty-three year old Paiute widow, and her half sister Lucille, age four. Lucille was listed as half Paiute, while Rosie and her mother were full Paiute. All three were born in Bodie. Katie's parents were born in Bridgeport, California. Katie earned money by doing housework such as laundry by the day. Laundry was typically done by hand using a washboard and tub.

The *Bridgeport Chronicle Union* reported that during the 1910 Fourth of July celebration, Rosie McDonald won $3.50 for first place in the "Squaw race", while Mrs. Dolan won the "Ladies race." A photograph of several festively dressed Paiute children crossing Main Street during the 1909 Fourth of July can be found in the book *Bodie "The Mines Are Looking Well"* (Piatt, 232). Perhaps one of them is twelve year old Rosie dressed in white.

When interviewed in 1979, Rosie Moose was described as a "wonderful gentle old Paiute woman" from Bishop, California. Rosie recalled living in the Indian House with her family when she was a little girl. She believed that her father had built the house. She recalled stopping by the J. S. Cain house each day after school and that often Mrs. Cain would have warm cookies ready to hand out to the children.

According to U.S. Indian Census data, they had moved to Bishop, California by 1913. Katie married Soda Tom in 1919. By 1921, Rosie had a son, Norman, and was Rosie McDonald Moose. Rosie had two more sons, Virgil and Nelson, and a daughter, Frances. Rosie and her family lived in Bishop most of their lives. Her grandson, Virgil Moose, who is the son of Nelson and Bertha Moose, is the Chairman of the Big Pine Paiute Tribe of the Owens Valley. Rosie's sons Virgil and Nelson have passed on and well as her half sister Lucille Encinas. Her daughter Frances, lives in Big Pine. Rosie was very special to her family and is held deeply in their hearts.

Indian House, Washtub, and Bird

Indian House

M. Y. S. KIRKWOOD

Michael Young Stewart Kirkwood was the owner of the Kirkwood house, and what is now known as the Stuart Kirkwood livery stable and blacksmith shop in Bodie. He was born in San Francisco on May 7th, 1863. His parents, Thomas and Susan Ann Kirkwood, were born in New Brunswick, Canada, and came to San Francisco "by way of the isthmus" the previous year. After trying mining in Aurora, they eventually settled on a 480 acre homestead in Bridgeport Valley in 1871, until 1915, when they moved to Orange, California. In 1910 they paid taxes on 50 head of cattle, 15 calves, a dozen chickens, harness, a dog, 10 work horses, 30 common horses, a milk cow, 30 tons of hay, and a hay press. They had seven children.

M. Y. S. Kirkwood apparently was named after Susan's brother, Michael Young Stewart, who was shipwrecked during a gale in 1850 on his way to the California gold fields. He was rescued, shipped back to Canada, and sailed again. Michael Stewart was the first sheriff of Mono County, when Aurora was the county seat. He was a proprietor of a restaurant in Bodie. M. Y. S. Kirkwood, who used the name Stewart as a first name, was a deputy sheriff and jailer. His horse's name was Convict. His brother Emery was a sheriff and tax collector. The April 11th, 1903 issue of the *Chronicle-Union* noted:

"Deputy Sheriff Kirkwood had the chain-gang at work on the streets, this week.
A very good scheme, Mr. Cop."

Kirkwood Blacksmith Shop

Like most Bodieites, Stewart tried prospecting. He also owned property in Bridgeport such as the Wolvereen Saloon and Bridgeport Market. He was the chairman of the board of supervisors for Mono County for many years, and commuted back and fort from Bodie to Bridgeport.

The 1920 Census shows M. Y. S. Kirkwood was 56 years old, divorced, and working in Bodie as a carpenter. He was living with his 13 year old adopted son, Orren. The blacksmith shop and livery stables first appear in tax records in 1928. Prior tax records seem to indicate there was an empty lot there. In 1925, Stewart Kirkwood bought the Travis building in Aurora and tore it down. Presumably, he used the building for building supplies. He died on April 3rd, 1946 in Bridgeport when he was 82 years old.

Kirkwood House

ROBERT CONWAY

Robert Conway bought and lived in what is now called the Conway House. The Green Street house still has some canvas cover left on one side of the building. Hops grow on the picket fence of the front porch, and used to grow half way up the canvas side. In the winter of 1943, he was one of only three people to live in Bodie, along with fellow caretakers Martin Gianettoni and Spence Gregory.

Thomas Robert Conway was born in East Hawkesbury, Ontario, on August 8th, 1875, and immigrated to the United States in 1898. He used the name for his official papers in Bodie, but was called Robert or Bob.

When Bob first arrived in Bodie, he worked on his older cousin Paddy's ranch. Bob's diaries indicated he did not like ranch work. By 1899, he joined the union and worked "in cyanide" at the Standard Mill.

In 1903, Bob went back to Ontario to marry Elizabeth Ann Mclaughlin on February 17th. In March, Bob and Annie Conway arrived in Bodie. They bought a house in August of 1903, from W. H. Osmun, a house painter, for five hundred dollars in gold. The house was on Green Street across from what would later become known as the Conway House, and is now called the Todd House. The Todd House collapsed in the winter of 1973-1974 and was reconstructed in 1999. In December of 1903, the *Chronicle Union* reported:

Todd and Conway Houses

"DIED, In Bodie December 10, 1903. The infant son of Robert and Annie Conway. -Aged 10 days
DIED, In Canada, Nov. 26. 1903, Andrew Conway, aged 70 years. Father of Robert Conway of this city.
Mr. Conways cup of sorrow is indeed full to overflowing losing in such a short space of time his father and his child. We tender to both he and his wife our condolence in their sad bereavement."

Dried Hops, Conway House

According to Canadian records, Robert's father Andrew was actually eighty years old when he died, Andrew and his older brothers, Gregory and John emigrated from Ireland to Ontario, Canada, and were farmers as was their father Gregory.

The same 1903 *Chronicle Union* newspaper reported that John Conway, Bob Conway's older cousin, and his family were leaving Bodie for a visit to Canada. John had just bought James Sturgeon's ranch for three thousand dollars in gold and would move his family to what would be called the Conway Ranch in the spring of 1904. The ranch, over a thousand acres on the northwest side of Mono Lake below what is now called the Conway Summit, was used to raise cattle and horses. The ranch remained in the family until the late 1970s, and later was bought by Mono County.

John's older brother Patrick, known as Paddy, owned a ranch in Sweetwater, Nevada, and was a partner with Johl and Donelley. He supplied livestock for their Bodie butcher operation. John and Paddy were also from East Hawkesbury and immigrated in 1878.

John Conway ran a blacksmith and wagon maker shop on Mill Street by Boone's Corral in Bodie. After moving back to Ontario and buying a farm there, his wife Catherine died during childbirth of their second child. He sold his Ontario farm, and moved back to Bodie. He married Catherine's older sister Mary back in Ontario in 1899 while he was visiting his first son. They moved back to Bodie. John and Mary's one year old child, George Washington Conway, died

Conway Bedroom

in 1901 of scarlet fever during the epidemic at the turn of the century, and is buried in Bodie. John was known as quite a dancer. He won a waltz contest in Bodie by dancing with a glass of water on his head (Kelsey). John died during the great influenza pandemic of 1918, and Patrick, who owned six thousand acres died in 1925 . They made their money initially as teamsters in the freight business, and left large estates. Another pioneer in Yosemite, named John Conway came from Pennsylvania was apparently not directly related.

Robert and Annie had three children: Dorothy Claire, born on December 17th, 1904 in Bodie, Charles Harold born on September 4th, 1907 in Bodie, and Mabel Margaret born on October 27th, 1911 in East Hawkesbury. Ontario.

Bob worked for the Standard Consolidated Mining Company in Bodie as a surface labourer and in the cyanide plant. In 1906, he worked in Manhattan, Nevada for six months. After moving back to Bodie, he worked

Conway Porch

as a machinist helper and pipe fitter until 1912. In Bodie, Bob enjoyed a good celebration as the May 20th, 1911, *Bridgeport Chronicle-Union* reported:

> "Bodie, May 19.—The Tommy Miller wedding last week was the occasion for the boys who believe in having a noise with their good time. Three battalions, in charge of Colonels Dick Hitchens, Frank Dolan and Bob Conway captured the town as neatly as Madero's insurrection took in the federals. The thirst quenching emporiums supplied joy water galore for the victors and all of them had a great time. "

In 1912, Bob worked in Calgary, Canada for several years where he did structural, concrete, and foundry work. He moved back and worked in Bodie and in the Nevada towns of Aurora, Wabuska, and Mason, and moved to Tonopoh in 1920 where he worked as a blacksmith and machinist helper for several years.

An article appeared in the newspaper titled "A Farewell Surprise", which told of a surprise party for Annie Conway and her children that was organized by Catherine Frack and Annie Miller. A luncheon was held at the Miners Union Hall which included dancing with piano and accordion music. The article stated "The party was the most enjoyable held in Bodie for a long time", and that Annie and her children would go to Tonopah to join Bob, while Dorothy would attend the excellent high school there.

Bob and Annie moved to Los Angeles where they bought a house in 1924, and sold their Bodie house and furniture to Ella Cain on January 19th, 1925. Bob worked as a pipe fitter there.

By 1927, Bob moved back to what he called "God's country", while Annie stayed in Los Angeles. Annie and her daughters attended a annual picnic in Long Beach for over sixty former Mono County residents. Bob worked on the Bodie roads, and as an election clerk for most elections. In 1930, Bob was living in Annie Miller's boarding house, and by 1931 he started paying taxes on the Conway House. Family notes indicate that the Conway house was a shell with no windows when he bought it.

Annie died on September 12, 1941 in a sanitarium in Los Angeles after living with her daughter, Mrs. Dorothy Daugherity. In his later years, Bob would winter in Bridgeport, Gardnerville, and other area hotels, and moved back to Bodie when the weather improved. In 1955, Bob was admitted to a sanitarium, and died in Los Angeles at the age of 81 on June 18th, 1957.

In 1967, the California Department of General Services contacted the heirs of Robert Conway regarding the transfer of their property in the Township of Bodie to the state. A Judgment of Condemnation was prepared and signed by Dorothy after an appraisal was conducted. The appraisal consisted of engineering, surveying, and inspecting. They requested permission from property owners to make the studies. The independent appraisers were hired to make an unbiased opinion of property value. Once the appraisal was completed they contacted the owners with a compensation amount. They determined that Dorothy and Harold, the living children and heirs of Thomas Robert Conway, would be compensated $250. The Judgment in Condemnation provided that all personal property must be removed within 90 days. Dorothy was unable to return to clean the rest of Bob's personal items from the house due to her husband's health, but most of his property was already cleaned out when it was evident that he was not returning to the house. The current contents of the house are the items left by Bob or the family.

Robert Conway Family Items

REFERENCES

Books

Billeb, Emil W. *Mining Camp Days.* Berkeley, CA: Howell-North Books, 1968: 205.
Cain, Ella. *The Story of Bodie.* San Francisco, CA: Fearson Publishers, 1956.
Calhoun, Margaret. *Pioneers of Mono Basin.* Copyright 1967 by Robert C. Calhoun
Geissinger, Terri Lynn. *Images of America Bodie 1859-1962.* San Francisco, CA: Arcadia Publishing, 2009: 47.
Hittman, Michael. *Wovoka and the Ghost Dance.* Lincoln, NE: University of Nebraska Press, 1997: 338.
James, Ronald M. and Raymond, Elizabeth C. *Comstock Women The Making of a Mining Community.* Reno, NV: University of Nevada Press, 1998: 223
Johnson, Russ and Ann. *The Ghost Town of Bodie a California State Park.* Bishop, CA: Chalfant Press, 1967: 38.
Kane, Elizabeth Wood. *Twelve Mormon Homes.* Philadelphia: William Wood, 1874.
Kelsey, Louise. *Here Come The Conways.* The Album, Vol V, No 2-3, Times & Tales of Inyo-Mono, Mono County Library
King, Larry R. *The Kings of the Kingdom, The Life of Thomas Rice King & his Family,* Orem, UT: 2008.
Leadbrand, Russ, Lowenkopf, Patterson, Bryce, *Yesterday's California,* Miami, FL: E. A. Seemann Publishing Inc, 1975:58.
Loose, Warren. *Bodie Bonanza,* Las Vegas, NV: Nevada Publications, 1989: 107-108.
McGrath, Roger D. *Gunfighters Highwaymen & Vigilantes,* Berkeley, CA: University of California Press, 1984: 156
Mack, Corbett, *Corbett Mack The Life of a Northern Paiute As told by Michael Hittman,* Lincoln, NE: University of Nebraska Press, 1996: 139, 215.
Merrell. Bill with David Carle, *Bodie's Boss Lawman,* Reno: Nevada Publications, 2003.
Penfield, Florence Bentz. *The Genealogy of the Descendants of Samuel Penfield,* Salem, MA: Higginson Book Co., 1963: 116.
Piatt, Michael H. *Bodie "The Mines Are Looking Well",* El Sobrante, CA: North Bay Books, 2003: 218-222, 255.
Poag, Larry. Guide to Shopkeepers and Shooters, Lake Grove, OR: Western Places, 1997.
Russell, Carl Parcher. *The Bodie that Was,* Touring Topics, November, 1929
Shamberger, Hugh A. *Candelaria and Its Neighbors,* Carson City, NV: Nevada Historical Press, 1978: 48.
Sprague, Marguerte. *Bodie's Gold,* Reno, NV: University of Nevada Press, 2003.
Spraker, Ella Hazel Atterbury, *The Boone Family,* Rutland Vermont, 1922
Ward. Maurine Carr. *Names of Persons and Sureties Indebted to the Perpetual Emigrating Fund Company from 1850 to 1877 Inclusive,* Salt Lake City, UT: Star Book and Job Printing Office, 1877: 208
Watson, James and Brodie, *Big Bad Bodie high sierra ghost town,* San Francisco, CA: Robert D. Reed Publishers, 2002
Wedertz, Frank S. *Bodie 1859-1900,* Bishop, CA,: Sierra Media Inc, 1969.
Williams, George III, *The Red Light Ladies of Virginia City Nevada,* Riverside, CA: The River Publishing, 1990.
Williams, George III. *Rosa May: The Search For a Mining Camp Legend,* Riverside, CA,: Tree By The River Publishing, 1984
Wilson, Neill C. *Silver Stampede,* Gioreta, NM: Rio Grande Press Inc., 1984
Yparraguirre, Frank. *An Interview with Frank Yparraguiree: A contribution to a survey of life in Carson Valley, from first settlement through the 1950s,* Reno, NV: University of Nevada Oral History Program, 1984: 115-116

Methodist Church Minutes:

California Conference, 1913, pp. 72-73, 78-79, George B. Hinkle
Southern California Conference, 1893, page 55, Fanny Lebus-Warrington
Southern California Conference, 1931, page 166, F. M. Warrington

World Wide Web Sources

www.ancestry.com *baptism, census, immigration, marriage, military, and passport records*
www.bodiehistory.com Bodie California History and Research, Michael Piatt
www.bonhams.com Bonhams and Butterfields
www.chroniclingamerica.loc.gov *Chronicling America, 1880-1922, San Francisco Call Bulletin*
www.familysearch.org *census records,* Latter Day Saints
www.freepatentsonline.com, Patent Search
www.fultonhistory.com *Bridgeport Chronicle-Union, Chronicle-Union, Poughkeepsie Eagle*
www.iavanburen.org Van Buren County Iowa GenWeb Project
www.newspaperArchive.com Newspaper Archive, *Oakland Tribune, Reno Evening Gazette, Hayward Daily Review*
www.sfpl.org San Francisco Public Library, *San Francisco Chronicle -1922*
www.willrogers.com *The Daily Telegrams of Will Rogers: # 1293*

Microform Sources

Mono County Library: *Bridgeport Chronicle-Union*
Doe Library, University of California at Berkeley: *Bodie Free Press, Bodie Morning News, Bodie Standard, Daily Bodie Standard*
San Francisco Public Library: *San Francisco Chronicle, New York Times*
University of Nevada at Reno: *Borax Miner*, *The True Fissure*, *Washoe Times*

Property Recordings

Mono County Recorder's Office, Bridgeport, CA
Esmeralda County Recorder's Office, Goldfield, NV
Tuolumne County Recorder's Office, Sonora, CA
Van Buren County Recorder's Office, Keosauqua, IA, by Donald W. Aldrich

Turned Wooden Globe

Special Collections

A.O.U.W. Bodie Lodge #143 Records, 1876-1912, Bancroft Library, University of California, Berkeley CA
Bodie Fraternal Burial Association Records, 1898-1908, Bancroft Library, University of California,
Baker, Mattie Mary. Scrapbook of undated news clippings, courtesy Robin Luke (great granddaughter of Lottie Johl).
Hoover, Mildred Brooke. *Reminiscences of Mildred Crew Brooke,* Hoover Institution Archives, Palo Alto, CA , 1940: 52
Hoover, Theodore J. *Memoranda : being a statement by an engineer,* Hoover Institution Archives, Palo Alto, CA, 1939: 129
Inventory of the County Archives of California : No. 27. Mono County, The Northern California Historical Records Survey Project, 1940, SF History Stacks, San Francisco Public Library, San Francisco, CA
I.O.O.F, Bodie Lodge Records, 1876-1916, Bancroft Library, University of California, Berkeley CA
Knights of Pythias, Mono Lodge, No. 59, Records : Bodie, Calif., 1879-1911, Bancroft Library, University of California, Berkeley CA
Mono County Records, Manuscript Collection, California History Section, California State Library, Sacramento, CA
Mono County Tax Records, Mono County Museum, Bridgeport, CA
Mono County (Calif.) Records, 1861-1918, Bancroft Library, University of California, Berkeley CA
Pioche Lodge No. 23 I.O.O.F. Collection, University Library, University of Nevada, Reno. (Boone & Wright)
Schwab family. *Schwab family genealogy collection*, P-388 - Johl Family, Center for Jewish History, New York, NY, 1980, courtesy Sondra S. Ettlinger

CPSIA information can be obtained
at www.ICGtesting.com
Printed in the USA
252630LV00002B